The Secret Diaries of Liam and Noel Gallagher

ALSO BY BRUNO VINCENT

Do Ants Have Arseholes? (co-writer)

The Secret Diary of Mario Balotelli

Danger Mouse Declassified

Five on Brexit Island

Five Give Up the Booze

Five Forget Mother's Day

Five Go Gluten Free

Five Go Parenting

Five Escape Brexit Island

Fairy Tales for Millennials

Sherlock Holmes and the Mystery of the Forgotten Password

Sherlock Holmes and the Case of the Trigger Warning

Sherlock Holmes and the Air Fryer of Doom

You Can't Say That Any More

The Secret Diaries of Liam and Noel Gallagher

an oasis parody

BRUNO VINCENT

C

CENTURY

CENTURY

UK | USA | Canada | Ireland | Australia
India | New Zealand | South Africa

Century is part of the Penguin Random House group of companies
whose addresses can be found at global.penguinrandomhouse.com.

Penguin Random House UK,
One, Embassy Gardens, 8 Viaduct Gardens, Nine Elms, London SW11 7BW

penguin.co.uk
global.penguinrandomhouse.com

Penguin Random House UK

First published 2025
001

Thanks to Clare Hodgson, Sophia Mangan and Henry Vincent

Illustrations by Emanuel Santos

Typeset in 12/15.6pt Garamond Premier Pro by Jouve (UK), Milton Keynes
Printed and bound in Great Britain by Clays Ltd, Elcograf S.p.A.

The authorised representative in the EEA is Penguin Random House Ireland,
Morrison Chambers, 32 Nassau Street, Dublin D02 YH68

A CIP catalogue record for this book is available from the British Library.

ISBN 9781529958492

Penguin Random House is committed to a sustainable future
for our business, our readers and our planet. This book is made
from Forest Stewardship Council® certified paper.

FSC www.fsc.org MIX Paper | Supporting responsible forestry FSC® C018179

This book is dedicated to the mysterious person who delivered the package of secret diaries to the editor, signing himself Damon A____ (the rest is a blur).

INTRODUCTION

On 3 April 2025, a mysterious cache of papers was discovered in a skip in Burnage, Manchester. Although not at first recognised, it was soon discovered to be a secret stash of private papers belonging to Oasis musicians Liam and Noel Gallagher, comprising lost diary entries from the brothers' early years, as well as more recent times.

The contents of the papers led us to think that these were parts cut out of the brothers' diaries. It seems likely that the pages were intended for destruction because the details contained within are personal, often controversial and offensive. And also, frankly, quite ridiculous.

With these papers were some other documents, including a mysterious piece of writing which appears to be a new work of religious literature: The Gospel According to Liam Gallagher.

Its authorship is unclear. It could be debated whether the person responsible was trying to start a new religion, taking the piss out of Liam Gallagher, or committing sacrilege to try to get themselves excommunicated from the Church and potentially assassinated by a religious fundamentalist. Possibly all three.

The documents are published here in their entirety, exactly as they were discovered.

The reader has been duly warned.

Sue Perssonick (editor)

22 September 1972 – NOEL (aged five)

Mam back from hospital today. Package in arms.

Brought home my new brother.

William John Paul Gallagher.

First impression, he's very immature.

No self-control.

Cries at the drop of a hat.

Total attention seeker.

Expects everything to be done for him.

Total baby.

29 September 1972 – NOEL

One week on.

Liam still crying. Mam says I have to share bedroom. Don't like this.

Tried to say to the lad there's certain house rules, but he don't listen.

Just cried and stuck his fist in his gob.

So apparently he's rude as well as being a slow learner.

Also Mam's obsessed with him and I'm getting no female attention.

Lad better grow up pretty quickly and show some respect.

Can't be putting up with this shit forever.

17 April 1973 – NOEL

Treated Our Kid to a performance of me new song.

Me on vocals and tambourine, with Paul on recorder. Still working on lyrics but has a working title of 'Woof Woof Brown Dog'.

Smashed it.

'What do you think?' I ask the little 'un. He just stares up at me, all stupid and dribbling.

Then the smell hits us.

'Gross!' I say, covering my nose.

'That's a bad review,' says Paul. 'Anyway, I still reckon it sounds too much like "Baa Baa Black Sheep".'

'Take that back!' I shout. 'It's original! I never copy other bands' music!'

THE GOSPEL ACCORDING TO

LIAM

Being the First Part

In the beginning was The Word. Which was on Channel 4 and did show the first ever Oasis TV appearance.

But our story starteth not there.

One night there came an ANGEL of the LORD into a humble dwelling in a place that was called Burnage, which was in the land of Manchester.

And the Angel did appear unto PEGGY GALLAGHER, and said to her: 'Be thou not afraid. For thou art of child.'

'Oh Jesus,' said Peggy.

'Yeah, 'fraid so,' said the Angel.

'A daughter this time, I hope?' she said. 'I've two boys already.'

'Thou shalt have a man child,' said the Angel.

'Oh Jesus,' sayeth Peggy again.

'OK, if you could just calm it down a bit on the blasphemy front,' said the Angel. 'Not to be a stickler but I am an ANGEL of the LORD after all.'

'Fair play,' said Peggy, performing the sign of the cross.

'But be not cast down and shed not your tears upon the earth,' went onneth the Angel, 'for he shall be famous in the land. I mean, really quite a nobhead at times. But then we all have our moments, don't we. But he will be truly mighty and win great acclaim among men.'

'Amen!' sayeth Peggy.

'No, I said "among men" – oh wait, Amen, yes. Sorry. Anyhonk – thus thou has been informed that a great person will be born in this house.'

'I think our Noel is talented also,' sayeth Peggy. 'And is perhaps a star in the making.'

'Yeah, no doubt,' saideth the Angel. 'Noel's no slouch. A bright lad. Two such will bring a great conflict into this house.'

'Are you kidding me?' quoth Peggy. 'It's conflict twenty-four-seven already.'

'As you were then,' sayeth the Angel. 'Please rate your experience with us today on this shining gold lozenge, from smiling angel to horned devil . . .'

1 May 1982 – LIAM

History teacher Mr Clement comes to me after class.

'Mr Gallagher, I'd like a word with you,' he says.

'Go on,' I say, quickly tucking the pack of fags I had just got out of my pocket into the inkwell.

'I was most interested in your essay, about the Industrial Revolution.'

'Nice one.'

'*Very* interested.'

'Yeah OK,' I say, shifting slightly in my seat.

'It was very insightful and well researched. You've never shown any promise in this class before, and I was most impressed.'

'OK, yeah well,' I say. Everyone else has filed out for break. Precious minutes ticking by. 'Er . . . Nice one,' I say again. 'You know, history and that. I'm mad fer it.'

'Can you tell me what the Corn Laws were?' he asks.

'Yeah.'

'Do go on.'

'Well,' I think, looking out of the window for a bit of the old inspiration. 'The Corn Laws, right, were – well, they was laws to stop shit jokes. You know. Stop people being corny.'

He nods, watching me. Normally there's a few other students around to lap this shit up, but with just the two of us I'm not enjoying myself quite so much.

'I see. And tell me – how would you explain the 1832 Reform Act?'

'How would I,' I say to myself. 'How would I.'

'Indeed.'

Why the fuck is this guy asking me so many questions? There's something bothering me in the back of my mind but I'm too worried trying to think about what the fucking Reform Law is.

'The Reform Law . . .' I begin.

'The Reform Act,' he says.

'Yeah, but I call it the law. That's what *I* call it.'

He narrows his eyes for a moment. 'Forgive me,' he says quietly. 'It *is* a law, after all.'

'Yeah, well before I was so rudely interrupted,' I go on. 'The Reform Law was to, uh, to make sure like that boys behaved themselves and didn't get sent to Reform School. That's what that was.'

Then he leans down, looking at me closely.

'I can see you're very shy about your considerable historical knowledge. You hate to show off, I can see that.'

This slightly makes my brain hurt, so I ignore it.

'Of course, the excellent essay that you handed in about the Corn Laws and the Reform Act really showed huge promise. I was surprised, in particular, because one of my pupils, whose essays are usually so excellent, refused to hand anything in on this topic at all. Young Peter Hopkins.'

'Oh right, Petey, what a shame,' I said. 'Lazy, is he?'

'Not usually, no. He loves history. And he turns up today, shivering and apparently terrified, and with a bruise on the side of his head, and his blazer torn, with no homework, and when I ask him why he's not done it he just turns white and shakes his head.'

'Poor lad,' I say. 'Maybe he's a bit soft.'

'And then here I have this essay, handed in by you – who, I can't help noting, has never actually handed in a single piece of homework ever, in this class. And it's a first-rate essay. That also happens to be speckled with blood. And to be written in Peter Hopkins's handwriting.'

He lets that sit. And stares at me.

I do the same. And stare back at him.

'Can you explain it?' he asks at last.

'The Lord moves in mysterious ways,' I say. 'And, er, you know. Wonders never cease.'

He nods. 'I'd like to read more of your history of Britain, Mr Gallagher. I'm sure it would be most entertaining. At detention each night this week. Now you may go.'

By which time break is nearly half over.

Nob.*

* See pp. 17, 64, 112 and 124 for Liam Gallagher's History of Britain.

27 September 1982 – NOEL

Get back to the bedroom I share with Liam tonight and he's uncharacteristically quiet. Seems like he's sulking.

'What's wrong, lad?' I ask.

He shows me a note.

'In trouble,' he says. The note's in Liam's handwriting:

Dear Headmaster, Liam wasn't in last three days he was sick and had the Bubonic Plaige. Sorry my handwriting looks like that of a ellevenn year old boy. Peggy Gallagher.

'Got caught out, eh?' I ask.

He nods.

'You want to know where you went wrong?' I ask.

He nods again.

'You're still only ten.'

1 October 1982 – NOEL

New term at school.

I'm there as little as possible, of course. Cos there's streets to roam and magic mushrooms to take. But got caught out at the end of last term, and so for a few days I'm keeping my head down and trying to stay out of trouble.

Only a couple more terms and I'll be out of here, get a job at our dad's concreting firm.

Then I hear a voice I recognise calling to me from a window.

It's our mam, who's started working at the school as a dinner lady. Which is annoying cos it makes it harder to skive.

But, y'know. Not impossible.*

'Noel,' she says. 'I'm watching Liam in the playground there. Something's going on. I don't like it. Keep an eye on the lad for me.'

I'm five years older than Our Kid and obviously I've got things I'd rather do than babysit. But family is family. Playground is a fucking jungle, where serious shit happens. Maybe keep half an eye out, would be for the best.

When I start looking, what I see is shocking.

At the end of school, I catch up Liam on the walk home.

'Oi, dickhead,' I say. 'How you doing?'

He's quiet, doesn't want to speak.

'Listen,' I say. 'School can be dangerous. At a boys' school especially. People act like animals. Bullying happens. We all see it. It leaves a lifelong scar, and can change people for the worse. But . . . I just want you to know, well, they *can* recover. And learn to survive.'

He walks along, hands in pockets. Refusing to speak.

* While his mother was a dinner lady at their school, for many weeks Noel went in just for lunch, to be seen by her.

'This doesn't last forever. Some little toe rags have got nothing more to do than bully and punch and hit. But when they leave and go into the world – I promise you, they get the life they deserve.'

Still he says nothing. Not looking up.

'Mam came to me and I saw what was going on with you. Listen, boys who get bullied are often the more sensitive and intelligent ones. Probably will go on to have good family lives and be valuable members of society. So it's important as your older brother that I tell you . . .'

He looks up at me at last and I think I see a flicker in his eyes.

'. . . you stop picking on those poor defenceless bastards or I'll smash your face in.'

26 December 1982 – LIAM

The Snowman on telly.

Creepiest thing I've ever seen in my life. Are they really showing this shit to young people?

So this kid wakes up and goes outside in the middle of the night and makes friends with a grown-up stranger what he's never met, who probably lives on the street. And this fucking idiot goes off with him on an 'adventure'.

Any kid that did that round here would need their head examined. They'd find him in the canal the next day.

Sick shit.

1 June 1983 – LIAM

I'm on final warning for not doing homework.

New teacher Mr Baxter's told us we've got to work out a business plan.

So, I work one out.

Pair of new Adidas trainers: £15
Pair of new Adidas trainers with five-finger discount: £0
Odds of going to prison if caught stealing: 15% (estimate)
Resale value of trainers to market stall trader: £2
Target amount: £35 to get junior season ticket for City
Number of trainers to steal to reach amount: 20 pairs

I hand this in and try to get out of the room before he reads it, expecting to get shouted at when he does. At the door I can't help looking back. Baxter's reading it, but instead of looking angry, he's smiling.

'Your maths needs work,' he says. 'But I'm impressed with your business sense. You're one of the only pupils who identified a genuine Manchester growth industry.'

At first I'm surprised, but then I look down and see that he's wearing a pair of brand-new Adidas trainers.

'Can I put you in touch with my brother?' he asks. 'He runs a market stall . . .'

14 February 1985 – NOEL

There's this brunette from school I've fancied for a year. Big brown eyes, sweet smile – Maureen O'Shea.

After three weeks of asking her out, she finally said yes. Took her for a walk around the park and then to the pictures. Made a date for her to come over here, and I came back to look at the place.

Bedroom with two teenage boys: needed tidying.

Got all the dirty clothes crammed into cupboards, hid most of the more childish toys that I could see. Want to look like a sophisticated man after all.

Stuck the Etch A Sketch under my bed, wrapped up the Meccano and Lego in some fish-and-chip paper and stuck it up the chimney. Chucked the crisp bags and sweet wrappers out the window. Ventilated a bit.

Liam's dirty pants I refuse to touch – I kicked them under his bed and saw something poking out. A bunch of papers, not in his handwriting. Couldn't help having a look. In fact the writing looked distinctly feminine.

What fell out was a pile of letters from girls. All different girls at that. I stared at them in disbelief.

I knew Our Kid was popular with the ladies. Every ten seconds the doorbell rings and someone asks, is Liam in. But here was evidence in black and white – well, blue, pink, purple and white, with hearts and kisses on every perfumed fucking sheet.

First my heart started to sink, then I started to panic. What's this? The handwriting on one of the notes was that of . . . Maureen O'Shea. And another – from her *older sister*. And another – from Mrs Connelly, Liam's fucking maths teacher!

I sat back on my heels, trying to take it all in.

Then the door to my bedroom opened and there was Maureen. She saw what was in my hands, and saw that I'd read it.

'I was hoping to steal those back when you weren't looking,' she admitted. 'I would have snogged you to get hold of 'em.'

'He's fucking twelve!' I said. 'You're seventeen!'

She just shrugged. 'He's got something.'

'Fucking syphilis probably, at this rate. Get out!' I shouted. But before she did, she grabbed her letters.

LIAM GALLAGHER'S HISTORY OF BRITAIN

Episode 1: Prehistory to 1066

c.3000 BC – Stonehenge

Basically better than the Egyptian pyramids, right, this bunch of hippies brought massive stones from like Wales or some shit, and stuck 'em up in line so you can watch the sun rise, right near Glastonbury (which shows they knew how to have fun, right), and they shagged and took drugs and that.

It was party central basically, best venue in Britain – sort of makes you think of the Hacienda in 1989.

Although you've got to say, it must've been raining most of the time – why didn't they concentrate on inventing bloody tents before they built the henges. And sanitary toilets, but then they still haven't figured that out in Glasto, have they.

But respect to the lads.

Stick it up the pharaohs.

80 AD – Boudicca

The Romans are in Britain and are being rude as fuck.

Horrible lads.

So this fit bird right (who's in her forties right, but still absolutely got it – think of like, I don't know, Sharon Horgan or Gillian Anderson or something) takes her kit off and paints herself blue, and then goes and fucks the Romans up.

I've seen a documentary about it.

The Romans have built a big city in London, and she comes from Norfolk, which in those days was probably less full of ignorant pig-fucking country bumpkins than it is today.

c. 600 AD – King Arthur

So there's this king who everyone thinks is amazing, but he doesn't seem to do much, just go looking for the Holy Grail.

But he never finds it.

And his best mate cops off with his missus.

And he's Welsh an' all. He's supposed to be buried in the middle of a holy lake but these days it's probably underneath a Sports Direct.

Yeah, so basically he's a bit shit.

Except, thinking on it, they must have had pretty amazing washerwomen in those days, cos it must have been a nightmare keeping them white uniforms clean when it's basically mud everywhere. And in the days before . . . you know, Daz and that.

Monty Python version is better, I reckon.

878 AD – King Alfred and the Cakes

So, this guy's the king right, and he's on the run cos some other fellers are trying to smash his face in.

And he's like, well hungry and that.

And he sees some woman has left some cakes to cool on her windowsill. And she's like proper working-class, right, probably has a whole bunch of mouths to feed.

But this king prick just comes up and helps himself to the cakes, yum yum. Maybe he's been on the green and has the munchies – I wouldn't put it past him, although they probably had some crap old version of weed in them days like dried daffodils or some shit.

Anyway, everyone's like, great mate, you fucking carry on. Eat all the cakes you like. Just cos he's a fucking king, what he's been born into.

Try that shit in Manchester and see where it gets you. A fucking punch in the mouth at very best.

Typical posh prat. Privilege innit.

Anyway, that's all he's known for, eating some fucking cakes, so fuck him. Was probably shit on the lute as well.

c. 1020 – King Cnut

This other king was fucked off with his advisors giving him all different advice all the time.

So he waded into the sea and said, look at me – can I push back the waves?

Cold swimming is really good for you, that's proven, so you've got to be impressed. He was ahead of the curve. An influencer if you will.

More than that of course, I've got to say what we're all thinking. Think of having a name like that and ending up being king – how he survived the playground alone. Talk about giving your enemies a break. And think of the graffiti. Let alone the . . . whatever, the ballads and that.

But he stuck it out and didn't get murdered so you've got to hand it to the lad.

King Cnut.

1066 – The Battle of Hastings

French blokes invade, and King Harold is caught out cos he just got invaded by the Vikings two weeks before, up in the North.

Has to march whole army south cos trains haven't been invented yet and so obviously everyone's knackered. Otherwise we would of mullered 'em.

King Harold gets an arrow in the eye, which is a nasty one. Should of gone to Ye Olde Specke Savers or something.

But he came down off the hill where he had the advantage and that gave the French a fighting chance. Bad mistake.

After that apparently the English became partly French or whatever, but not me.

14 April 1985 – NOEL

Weird dreams of being attacked by a metal machine that looked like the Terminator.

As it got closer I saw it had Liam's face.

Couldn't escape. Felt its metallic arms reaching out and trying to strangle me.

Woke up, yelling – to find there was a fucking pushbike on top of me.

Other side of the room, there's Our Kid whistling as he takes his trousers off.

Me: 'What the fuck!'

Him: 'Oh, you're awake.'

Me: 'Course I'm fucking awake, there's half a ton of metal on my face!'

He shrugs. Does he help me get out from under it? Does he fuck.

I struggle free and nearly have an eye ripped open on the gears. I can't believe he's dumped a bike on me.

'Where did you get this?' I say, pushing one of the pedals out of my groin.

'Found it,' he says.

'Why is it here? And on me?'

'Didn't want anyone to come looking for it.'

I clear my throat. 'And why, if it's not too much to ask? Seeing as I'm speaking to the new fucking fitness expert of the Greater Manchester area?'

'You heard the speech that Tory bloke Tebbit made. If you're unemployed, get on your bike. So I did.'

'Except it's not your bike,' I say.

'Is now,' he says.

'That's where you're wrong. You dumped it on my bed. It's *my* bike now. So you'd better get on your bike – metaphorically speaking – and go and nick another fucking bike.'

But he's already asleep.

23 January 1986 – LIAM

Letter arrived today, from the BBC. All on official paper and that.

'Dear Mr Gallagher,' it says. 'Thank you very much for writing to apply for Jim to Fix It for You. Unfortunately we were unable to invite you to come on the programme. I'm sure you understand we receive hundreds if not thousands of letters every week, and although we'd love to, it's simply not possible for all those young people who are kind enough to write in to be invited onto the programme. Please keep watching! With best wishes from the *Jim'll Fix It* Production Team.'

Why'd they bother writing back like that? Might as well just send a postcard with 'fuck off, kid' on it.

Out of the letter flutters a little handwritten note.

'Just so you know,' it says, 'we thought your letter was the best one we've ever received, and it would have made us very happy to make your dream come true. It would have to be broadcast after the watershed, of course. But still, many of us who work here would have loved to watch you "break every bone in Jimmy's body with a hammer before setting fire to his balls and feeding him into a wood chipper".'

2 February 1986 – NOEL

Liam says there's a new English teacher at school.

Good luck to her, with that bunch of animals.

He comes home today and says she's trying to get them to read *Oranges Are Not the Only Fruit*.

I don't stop laughing for five minutes.

'I mean, what is that shit, as a title?' he keeps saying. 'It's got to be the worst title of all fucking time, right? Might as well call it *Eating Sausages Every Night Makes You Lardy*. Or . . . *Tony Blackburn is a Prick*.'

He can't get over it. I'm trying to read, as it happens. A biography of Neil Young. Can't get through a single line with him going on like this.

'It's fuckin' mental,' he says. '*Falling Over Backwards You Can Really Hurt Your Arse*. That would be a better title.'

'Liam,' I say quietly. 'Do you know what that book is about?'

'Two hundred pages,' he says, flicking through it. 'Published by a bunch of demented fuckheads.'

'I mean, do you know about the *theme* and *contents* of the book?' I ask.

He turns it over in his hand. 'Making fruit salad maybe.' Then he squints at me. 'What the fuck are you going on about?'

I tell him what it's about.

Several hours of glorious silence. I've never seen him read so fast.

3 February 1986 – LIAM

Got to school, every lad in the playground is dog-tired.

Word got about. They all heard what *Orange Is Not the Only Fruit Flavour* is about as well.

Every bastard stayed up all night reading it.

We all agree. Worst fucking lesbian porn ever written.

Hardly a single bare knocker in the whole thing.

Fucking dogshit.

10 January 1987 – NOEL

This is no kind of life. Sharing a bedroom with teenage Liam, then working all day at our dad's concrete business.

Hour after hour in an environment of shouting, swearing and imminent physical danger. The dust, the smell, the masculine bravado.

It's a relief to leave it all behind and go to the building site.

17 January 1987 – NOEL

Had an idea for a song during the day working at the concrete firm. When I get home I want to write it down as quickly as possible.

Can't find my guitar anywhere.

After stomping round the house for ages, find it neck down in the downstairs loo.

What the fuck is this? Take it out and wash it off. Dry it. Not amused.

When I start playing it, I can't get a good sound out of it. I inspect it all over, looking for cracks. Dead scared – if this thing's broken I can't afford to replace it.

Can't find anything wrong. Start playing again, still a weird sound. Then, I hear something rattling inside.

Carefully taking it out, I see that it's a piece of scrunched-up paper. I unfold it to see what it is. A letter.

'Dear Liam,' it begins.

'I'm delighted to offer you the opportunity to come to appear on *Stars in Their Eyes*, performing as Boy George. Your loving brother Noel wrote to us, explaining your hardship. How appalling that you lost both your legs and your genitals in a threshing machine. We will send a car for you on the day of your choosing and of course be able to accommodate your colostomy bag. A nurse will be provided for your personal care for the whole day. We look forward to meeting you. You are very brave.

Yours sincerely,

Leslie Crowther.'

On the bottom of the note is written in Liam's writing: **Your lucky I didn't cut the strings you cunt.**

Reading it, I'm impressed. I didn't write any letter. Long time since I've been so properly stitched up by me brother Paul. Respect.

15 October 1987 – NOEL

After Michael Fish said on the news that there was going to be no hurricane, well, what do you know. Biggest hurricane in the world just hit.

'Fuckin' hurricane can have it,' says Liam. 'Why doesn't it fuck off? I'm trying to sleep!'

'Go and beat it up then,' I say from my bed.

'I fuckin' will an' all!' He throws open the window. 'Go on, fuck off!' Then he stomps downstairs and into the street.

A destructive, relentless force of nature, the likes of which the British Isles have not seen in a generation.

Going outside to argue with a hurricane.

I feel sorry for the hurricane.

30 March 1989 – NOEL

Can't sleep.

Liam won't shut up, talking to me or to himself. Fourteen years of sharing a bedroom, and he still can't give me a moment's peace.

Stupid that I have to share a room with a fucking moody teenage kid. Got to move out.

I say: 'Why don't we both come up with our ultimate football teams.'

Then there's quiet in the room for half an hour, while we both think.

Finally I've come up with my team.

Lying there in the dark, I can see them all on the pitch together. Peter Shilton. Stuart Pearce. Ian Rush. Terry Butcher. Ian Wright. Paul Gascoigne. Peter Beardsley. John Barnes . . .

I'm interrupted by him laughing.

'Come on then,' I say. 'Who's on your fucking team then?'

'Rambo,' he says. 'Steve McQueen.'

'What is this, *Escape to* fucking *Victory*?'

'I haven't finished,' he says. 'I've also got Maggie Thatcher. Samantha Fox. A skip. Four of them soldiers from Afghanistan. What are they called?'

'The Mujahideen?'

'Yeah, them. And a llama.'

'What the fuck are you talking about?'

'That's my team. You said this was fantasy football.'

'You can't have a fucking *skip*.'

'Skip's going in goal. Park it up in the goalmouth, block it out all nice.'

'Right. Go on. I'm interested in this now.'

'Cos you've got Gazza, right. And he's pretty amazing. Can bend the ball. Score from half a mile. But I'm thinking even he can't get it in round a fucking skip. Know what I mean?'

'OK, I'm still listening. So, you've got Maggie Thatcher and Samantha Fox, right? Want to explain that?'

'Right. Cos I reckon no one could be on a football pitch with Maggie Thatcher without wanting to kick her head in, right?'

'OK. Well . . . that's probably true.'

'So half your players are kicking Maggie Thatcher's head in. Half are looking at Samantha Fox's tits. Right? And then half are watching Rambo go up against the Afghanistan fellers. Blood everywhere, right. And Rambo's got a bazooka.'

'He has indeed. Unless Peter Beardsley robs him of it.'

'I think he'd take Beardo out early doors. Anyway, all my players are distracting your players.'

'Or blowing them to smithereens or flashing tits at them.'

'Right. And then there's Steve McQueen riding his motorbike down the pitch to pass to me. And there's me up front. Forgot to mention that. Scoring goals.'

‘So you’re not intending to win the match with football skills then? An actual game of football?’

‘You’re just a fucking square. You always were. Don’t understand the rules of your own game. It’s not football. It’s fantasy football. Might give myself the ability to shoot thunderbolts out my arse as well. *Fantasy*, mate. You turned up against Rambo and Thatcher and Steve McQueen with a bunch of puny-arsed footballers.’

I admit to myself he’s got a point.

Our Kid can be funny at times.

THE GOSPEL ACCORDING TO
LIAM

Being the Second Part

At that time which the ANGEL did foretell, in the Year of Our Lord 1972, there came a light in the sky above Manchester.

And many did look at it and wonder what it did portend.

And someone did say, is it a new star in the night sky?

And others did say, or is that BHS burning down?

And yet others who did have wisdom in their hearts did say – no, smell that, it's a mattress fire in Burnage.

When Peggy grew large with child, and her time was upon her, three wise men appeared from the East.

'We have travelled from the East,' the first one said.

'Oldham,' said the second.

'We saw the bright light in the sky and did follow it,' said the third. 'For many days and nights. (Actually just over an hour, cos of the one-way system for camels.)'

'And thus we followed the signal even unto this place,' said the first. Cos it seemed they politely took it in turns to speak, being wise.

They came laden with gifts.

One had brought some Newcastle Brown Ale.

One had brought a bottle of knock-off perfume from the market, what had a posh label but smelled like a French house for women of ill repute.

The third had brought some tiny trainers and a little baby parka to lay at the feet of the infant. And everyone who saw these did say, 'Awwwwwwwwwwwww.'

The boy was born and was called William John Paul George Ringo Gallagher, for he was named after his patron saints who were of great fame and were of the nearby land of Liverpool.

He grew up into a youth.

Liam left school and went into the world of men (being not a natural scholar).

And he did work on a building site, where his brother had been injured by a gas main falling on his foot, and been on the sick for three months.

Whereupon the brother (whose name was NOEL) was given a safe job in a store cupboard where he was able to sit with a guitar all day and write songs.

But at that time Liam had received no such injury, although many there were in the land who might have gladly volunteered to give him such. For he had on him a mouth and a half.

It came that the young Liam was expected to lay cement. And do general labouring.

And he did find it boring, and did fuck it off.

15 April 1989 — NOEL

I'm in the middle of writing a song at my flat when there's a knock on the door and Liam comes crashing in, making loads of noise as always. He slams the wardrobe door, throws his trainers across the room into the corner.

I was just getting somewhere, and now the chorus has gone right out of my head.

'That's another fuckin' *Kubla Khan* moment,' I say under my breath. Stupid idea – I know he won't get the reference, and he'll not let it go.

'What the fuck's that?' he says.

'Kubla Khan,' I say. 'Indian place in the city centre. Famously noisy innit. Why don't you go out and get me some tandoori chicken.'

'Not hungry,' he says. Then: 'What's all this I keep hearin' about Chananmen Square.'

The song has nearly completely gone out of my head.

'What?' I say. He repeats hisself. He means Tiananmen Square.

'Chinese restaurant,' I say. 'Really good apparently. Explosive reviews. They don't like students though.'

'Give us a quid then, and I'll go out and get some fried rice.'

'You just said you weren't hungry,' I say, wary of getting my hopes up. Maybe the song isn't gone after all. And I've got a quid . . .

'I changed my mind,' he says. 'I'm hungry for Chinese. Where is it?'

'Right the way across town. It's worth it though. Ask any Chinese person you meet, they'll be glad to help you.' I toss him a quid. He fucks off. I think of trying to wind him up about his clothes – but no one on earth would ever mistake that ragamuffin for a student.

He's been gone for hours. He's probably dead by now, murdered by the offended Chinese population of Manchester.

Wrote two songs.

Heaven.

17 April 1989 – NOEL

Liam finally came back after two days of looking for Tiananmen Square, with a black eye. Won't talk about what happened.

9 November 1989 – LIAM

Everyone keeps talking about the Berlin Wall falling down.

Pathetic. If you're going to build a wall, build it proper so it doesn't never fall down. Our uncle Kev would of built it proper.

12 November 1989 – NOEL

Our Kid talking shite about the Berlin Wall being badly built.

Try to explain to him about the concept of freedom and how it's been denied to half a billion East Europeans since the 1950s. How this event means that tyrants and despots are being overthrown.

Now real life can begin for these people who were trapped under the yoke of communism. I tell him the Berlin Wall is the most important one in the world right now. Even more than the Great Wall of China.

I can see he's not listening.

'I know what you would do if you could,' I say. 'You'd go down the old bomb site and nick some rubble and tip it in a shopping trolley and flog it from a market stall to tourists. You'd probably put on a shit German accent like in *'Allo 'Allo!* and change your name to Liam Von Trapp, claiming to be just arrived from East Germany.'

He goes quiet, thinking for a bit.

Sometimes you can hear his brain working so loud like it's a rusty cuckoo clock winding up for a chime.

Next day and the day after he's nowhere to be seen. Finally he comes back with a grumpy expression and a bump on his head.

'Tourists of Manchester saw through you and fought back when you refused to offer discounts?' I ask.

'Fuck off,' he says.

Looking forward to going back on tour with the Inspiral Carpets. So I don't have to put up with this shit anymore.

31 December 1989 – LIAM

Noel won't shut up about the historical importance of the Berlin Wall. Stopped listening to him as usual, just let it wash over me.

Makes me think – when I saw that Stone Roses gig, and saw Ian Brown strutting around that stage, I realised that being a singer maybe isn't just a job for stupid ponces. There he was looking proper fucking cool and getting people's respect.

Hadn't thought about it much more until today.

Seeing David Hasselhoff singing on top of the Berlin Wall, the last piece of the puzzle falls into place. I realise the truth.

If you're a rock star you can command people's respect, and *also* get to work with Pamela Anderson in a red one-piece swimsuit.

THE GOSPEL ACCORDING TO

LIAM

Being the Third Part

However, a time came whenst the brother NOEL was taken into a different land, to be a guitar tech and roadie for the Inspiral Carpets.

Who were apparently a big deal at the time but, seriously, who the fuck has heard of 'em except in this context. This being a rhetorical question of the LORD.

Noel did travel long among the Far Places of the Earth, like even unto Japan and shit, and did make divers contacts in the Music Industry.

And at last, after many journeys, did he phoneth his mother from Munich and ask how she was getting on, and she did say she missedeth him and hoped he was keeping his underpants clean, mothers being what they are. And almost as an afterthought Noel did ask what his younger brother was getting up to.

'He's out right now,' said Peggy. 'Rehearsing.'

'Rehearsing what?' asked Noel. And a spirit of incredulousness was upon him. For the infant Liam that was known to him had been a feckless youth who stuck at nothing and certainly had no apparent musical leanings whatsoever.

'Rehearsing in a band,' sayeth Peggy.

'A fucking BAND?' asked Noel. And his mother did admonish his wicked tongue. But Noel's curiosity was set aflame.

For, forsooth, he could not picture Liam being in a band that was anything except a consummate load of dogshite.

In this time, as were all the lands in the North of England, the Land of Manchester was suffering with poverty, unemployment and hopelessness, and generally shit opportunities for young men. Such that the wisdom was that the only chances for employment lay in football, construction and drug dealing.

And into this barren place was born a guitar band of Working-Class youths called Guigsy and Bonehead and Tony McCarroll and Chris

Hutton. And the band was called The Rain.

And even as it had been foretold by the prophet Noel, they were a consummate load of dogshite.

They did meet at a public house called the Monarch. And didst only have a drum machine and a singer who couldst not remember the words of their songs.

And then the youthful Liam did appear, and they did sack their previous singer, which was sad and awkward as they were all childhood friends.

And The Rain did continue rehearsing for a year with Liam as frontman, for all did agree he had stage presence.

But they did hardly do a handful of gigs. Which were as sparsely attended as there are figs upon the fig tree that does dwell in the desert and appeareth to be dead or on its last bloody legs.

The Rain did change their name to Oasis, for it was agreed The Rain was a depressing and rubbish name for a band from Manchester.

But the music, despite a good sound and a lot of attitude, did not really turn anyone's head, even the band's loved ones who came along and wanted to give them a break.

And then Noel did come to see them, and the youth Liam was excited for his older brother's approval. But approval he did withhold, saying when Liam did ask him, witheringly: what a load of shit.

But Bonehead did notice Noel tapping his foot and talking excitedly to people. And did know that he was impressed but pretended to hate them. Because the spirit of the dickhead was upon him.

Oasis said to Noel, why not be our manager?

And he said: no.

Oasis said to Noel: but with your contacts we could really make something here.

And Noel said: nah, fuck it, I'm busy.

And Oasis did talk among themselves. And Liam did say to Bonehead, why don't we fire Guigsy and get Noel as rhythm guitar? And Bonehead gave him a hard look and Liam knew he had stepped in shit – and truly he felt ASHAMED. And never again suggested such a thing.

Then Oasis came again to Noel and said: you've got some songs, right? Come down and play them with us?

Noel said: too fucking right I have.

And he did play them. And when Oasis heard them they thought: holy shit these are good, we've already got a sound but with these songs we could really do something good.

And hearing the band play his songs, which he had only ever played in his bedroom on his guitar, Noel did have a Mancunian conversion there and then, and knew he wanted to do nothing else for the rest of his life.

And then their first gig did approach, and only the night before, Noel did realise he'd literally never played the guitar standing up before, and only had twenty-four hours to learn how to do so, and even before that he had to find somewhere to buy a guitar strap.

And he did shit his pants.

13 March 1992 – LIAM

Got told we couldn't rehearse at the local hotel anymore. The barmaids got caught out giving us too many freebies. Was good while it lasted.

Got to rehearse somewhere. After talking about it, the lads decided we'd go to the Boardwalk in central Manchester. But we had to pay. And none of us could afford it.

But we went in to have a look anyway.

The lads all reckoned this was the cheapest rehearsal space we'd find anywhere in Manc.

It wasn't so bad. We all agreed. Other bands in other rooms making plenty of noise.

Bonehead had one look around and pointed to the corner.

'They'll want that plastering,' he said. There was a juicy crack all the way up the wall.

'And here,' said Tony McCarroll. 'Look at that.' There was a gaping hole in another corner, where someone had smashed something into it.

Within minutes we were upstairs making a deal.

'Bonehead's the best plasterer around,' I said. 'We'll fix up that downstairs room for free – if you let us rehearse.'

Manager said yes.

So Bonehead fixed it up and painted it so it was like new. And we were in there twice a week for two months.

Then a few weeks ago they start asking for money again and we've got none – we're still signing on for fuck's sake.

So I go looking around in the downstairs corridor.

Come back a minute later.

'There's a door off its hinges down there,' I say to the manager. 'And a pipe broken, that's leaking pretty bad. Bonehead could help you out with both of those.'

Guigsy gives me a suspicious look.

There is, I admit, a splash of water from the pipe on my trousers. And a few splinters from the shattered door in my hair.

Bonehead keeps a straight face. Manager agrees to the deal. But when he's gone, Bonehead corners me.

'You thick cunt, I'm not a carpenter or a plumber. Stop giving me jobs I'm not trained for.'

'Thinking on my feet, Bony!' I say. 'Besides, you're a bright lad, you'll figure it out. We all believe in yer!'

He's not happy but he eventually calms down.

Pretty sure I can keep this thing going. At least this way we've got a place to rehearse.

Then today, I'm just coming round the corner of the street and the manager of the Boardwalk spots me and runs over. He looks scared as fuck.

'Listen, Liam,' he says. 'You can have the rehearsal space for free, right? I give in! Just please do me a favour and stop smashing shit up! This is my livelihood, man!'

13 December 1993 – LIAM

Rehearsals been good with the band.

Gigs we've done are going well, but the bunce is still only enough to keep us in lager and white powder. We're all still signing on and also doing shifts for our mate Bigun's* business – valeting posh cars in Manchester.

Bigun had a stroke of genius. Drove up to Trafford Park and offered to clean Alex Ferguson's car for free, so long as he could have a contract to valet all the Man U players' cars. Said yes on the spot.

But it's starting to bum us out that we're now doing all the United players' cars on a weekly basis, all these Porsches and Ferraris.

Thing is, of course, we fucking hate Man U.

'Eh, Bigun,' I say. 'We all fucking hate Man United. Why can't we valet the cars for Man City?'

He's surprised.

'I thought you'd want to do the expensive cars for the famous players. Big rock star like you wants to be driving Maseratis round the city, no?'

'But we're fucking Man City fans, man!'

He shrugs. 'OK. My pleasure. Be my guest!'

* Paul Ashbee, important friend to the founding members of The Rain/ Oasis.

20 December 1993 – LIAM

Caught up with Bigun in the pub.

'Eh, Bigun,' I say. 'Do me a fucking favour. Get me taken off doing these Man City cars, will yer?'

I was expecting him to look surprised. But this time he just fixes me with a level stare. 'Why's that, Liam?' he says.

'I can't be seen cleaning these fucking Minis and beat-up Ford Escorts, man! It's depressing as fuck, it's killing me out there!'

'Want to work on the United cars again, then?'

'Yeah,' I say. 'But like, don't tell anyone.'

'Anyone ever told you you're an annoying fucker, Liam?' he asks.

'Dunno. They might of done, but I wasn't listening,' I say. 'There's a good lad, Bigun. Maseratis again, eh?'

He nods, looking tired.

18 February 1994 – NOEL

Never like Channel crossings. Can't get to sleep. Pass out for a few moments, then wake up when my paperback biography of Brian Epstein falls onto my face.

Massive gig, the biggest we've ever had. Supporting The Verve in Amsterdam. The next step in the masterplan.

We've just got to make sure we take advantage of every opportunity like this. Stay the course. And we'll be a giant band. Maybe the biggest band in Britain. Maybe the world . . .

I realise I've finally fallen asleep for real when I wake up and the boat's still. I know we're at the other end.

Gonna be a big day, a huge gig for us. Adrenaline pulsing in my veins.

Go up on deck to find no sign of the other band members. Then a guard approaches me.

'Please sir, will you be coming to the brig to identify some prisoners?'

'Alright,' I say. 'What the fuck's a brig? Are we in a pirate film or som't? Where's fucking Errol Flynn?'

I've been following him through various corridors, and finally find myself looking at a bunch of vomit-strewn reprobates in the ship's metal cage of a prison.

Which, by the way, is the brig.

'Our Kid's here,' says Liam. The others turn over from where they've been sleeping like murdered corpses in the corner.

It occurs to me that building the most famous rock and roll band in the world is more complicated than writing and performing songs, and recording albums.

'You will be deported without setting foot upon Dutch soil,' says the officer. 'You will be transported back to Britain and released into the custody of the British police. As a matter of fact, I've already heard the story being broadcast on the ship's radio. So the media are aware of this international incident.'

'Alright, Vincent van Dickface,' I say. 'We've got your message.'

My plans are in tatters. Our first and maybe only chance to play a big international gig. Everything we've worked for over the last three years is ruined. Gone for what – a fucking punch-up with some drunk dickheads . . .

18 February 1994 – LIAM

Ferry trip to Amsterdam.

Chased by police. Ran away. Some stuff got broke.

Bit of a fracas.

Slight argy-bargy.

Noel mithering for some reason. Whiny little dwarf.

In the end we got turned back and came straight home again. Proper holiday – didn't have to sing to any of those weird canal-loving clog-sucking dyke-fingerers.

Fuckin' have it.

THE GOSPEL ACCORDING TO
LIAM

Being the Fourth Part

And there was a time when Liam was at a wedding feast in Chorley. A great celebration and a time of merriment.

But the revellers at the feast did come to Liam and say: oh woe is us, for we have no more wine.

And Liam did see that the wine had indeed run out, and there was great sorrow all around.

And he saw the guests had turned to him in their time of need, for the wedding feast was in danger of being ruined.

Show me your money, sayeth Liam.

And they did so.

And Liam said, now look, for I have turned your money into white powder. And they did say unto him, for sure you have saved the best until last, for this is some strong shit! Truly he is a worker of miracles!

The word of his works did spread amongst the land.

And Liam did say: as you were.

And a great Opportunity did arrive for the young band Oasis, which was to play a gig at King Tut's Wah Wah Hut in the Land of the Scots.

They got the gig on the word of a friend's band, who were also booked in the same venue and who said it was OK and that they were sure to get on.

(So basically they were chancing it.)

(Which shows the sort of youthful guts, zeal and chutzpah that were to become their trademark.)

(But still, gutsy as fuck. They hired a van with their dole money, on the bloody off chance!)

The venue, being in the City of Glasgow, was a six-hour drive from Burnage, and the band did arrive to discover that the venue did not have a licence (owing to some new bullshit local ordnance) for more than three bands per night, and they did already have three bands on the bill.

The venue did say: do the maths, lads. You're not going on.

Liam did make some thoughtful suggestions about the rearrangement of the bouncer's facial features, and his acolytes did also make some helpful points, which may or may not have entirely helped matters. And at the end the management did yearn for a quiet life and allowed Oasis to play three songs.

And there was a Powerful Man of the Music Industry in the Land of the Scots that day by the name of ALAN MCGEE, of Creation Records, who was there to see his friend's band, and he had drunk four JD and Cokes, and waxed enthusiastic.

And when Oasis did play their first song, McGee thought to himself: these guys are amazing, but maybe it's the JD speaking.

And when Oasis did play their second song, McGee thought to himself: I think I want to sign these guys. But he did stay his hand.

And then Oasis did play 'I Am the Walrus', which is always their closer to this day, and McGee did decide that this was the next biggest band in Britain.

And McGee did go over to tell them so. And Noel did say, do you want to hear our demo, and did hand him a tape, and McGee said, not really, I want to sign you. But did take the tape anyway. (Of which there are apparently only five copies, some of which are missing, and you can only imagine what they might fetch on eBay.)

And Noel said, alright, sounds good to me.

Although technically they did not actually sign to Creation but to Sony Records because of share buyouts and stuff but whatever.

And there was a powerful new musical force in the land.

3 August 1994 – NOEL

Back in Manchester.

Going into town to see Johnny Marr.

Can't believe we're mates. Always been a massive fan, and now all of a sudden I'm going to his house to play him some of my new stuff, and apparently he's got a guitar to give me. Fucking surreal.

Just weeks ago I was signing on. As I have that thought, I go past the Job Centre.

Happen to look in and I see Liam.

Kind of shocked. The album's finished. It's due out at the end of the month.

McGee reckons it's going to sell twenty million copies – and Our Kid is still signing on. If we do sell millions, I'll make maybe ten times what Our Kid does. I've got songwriting royalties, rest of the lads just get performing royalties.

Unless we start filling stadiums soon, I guess even with performing fees right now he's earning a lot less than a plumber.

We don't know for sure if it will sell anything. Nothing's guaranteed in this world.

Shit. Maybe I should still be signing on too.

3 August 1994 – LIAM

Down Job Centre earlier.

Another appointment with the dark-haired sort in the corner office.

She looks up when I come in.

'Mr Gallagher, sit down.'

'Alright,' I say.

'I've been seeing you for a few years now,' she says, looking at my file.

She's got this wavy long hair and this feminine physique with all curves exactly where they should be. And nice nails and that. With the album out in a few weeks I won't be back, so I've decided I'm going to ask her out once and for all.

'When you first visited me you said you could not find work because there's no positions at the moment for astronauts.'

'Correct,' I say.

'I trust you have not yet found a mission to suit your talents?'

'Well, I've had a bit of a career change,' I say.

'I know you have,' she says, flicking through the pages. 'More than one, in fact. Next time I saw you, you claimed to be in the SAS. You said you got kicked out of the SAS for being, and I quote, "too good at slotting hostiles and making the other dickheads look lazy, but they hated to see me go cos they all loved me". And you were therefore unable to find employment as a soldier.'

'Also correct,' I say. 'But there's been a bit of a change of circumstances . . .'

'I'm not surprised,' she said. 'Your career has been remarkably varied. Most recently you claimed you could not get work because there were no places for submarine commanders in Manchester, owing to it being landlocked.'

'Well it is,' I say. 'That is unarguable. A fact what I only discovered too late.'

'So how may I help you today?' she asks.

And she looks at me with that little sceptical squint that makes her eyes really pretty.

'Had another career change,' I say. 'I'm now the greatest rock star in the world.'

And I go to put me feet up on her desk but decide it's a bit much in a public office with people looking in (thought I saw Noel driving past outside earlier) so I stick 'em on a chair instead.

'Oh indeed,' she says.

'Yeah,' I say. 'So I wondered if you'd like to go and get a bottle of champers, on me.'

'As a matter of fact,' she says, looking at me proper for the first time, 'it was always my dream to go out with a rock star.'

'Alright then,' I say. 'Now we're getting somewhere.'

'Unfortunately, the only people I meet seem to be hopeless liars and bullshit artists who waste my time. I assume with your new-found riches you'll be signing off. Good luck. Now, if you would please leave, my next appointment is due.'

1 November 1994 – NOEL

One of the most amazing evenings of my life.

Coming off stage, someone says to me: 'Noel, there's someone here I thought you'd like to meet . . .'

Next thing I know I'm shaking hands with Paul McCartney. I'm dazed, don't know what to say. It's so noisy we can hardly hear each other talk.

'Here, come back to my dressing room for a moment, Paul,' I say.

We chat as we walk backstage.

'I think it's really unfair how people have labelled you a bunch of violent yobs,' says Paul. 'Just because you're working-class musicians, like The Beatles were in the sixties.'

'Thanks, Paul,' I say.

'I can tell from listening to your music that you're an intelligent artist who's surrounded himself with like-minded talented people,' he goes on.

'I'm glad you think so,' I say. 'Come and meet the other members of the band.'

I open the door to the dressing room. There's a bald bloke with a half-drunk bottle of vodka in his hand, having his face repeatedly smashed into the door of a cupboard by a tall feller.

'Steal fifty quid off me, would you, you cunt?' the tall feller is saying. 'I needed that for speed!'

'Allow me to introduce you to Bonehead and Bigun,' I say.

10 December 1995 – NOEL

Press conference today. I'm surprised by a sudden flashback to my childhood.

'Mr Gallagher,' says a journalist to me. 'Obviously your brother is a brilliant singer, and you are acclaimed as one of the greatest songwriters of your generation. Is there any music in your genes, do you think?'

Suddenly I'm transported back to Manchester in the late seventies and early eighties. To the rainy Friday and Saturday nights when we little ones would be dragged to the smoky pubs and clubs.

Watching two hundred people swaying and singing along to the 1940s and '50s country and western records my dad was playing. As a DJ, this was his patch, playing country and western to Irish immigrants in the North East. The one release at the end of their week, in those disgusting, stinky dens filled with shouting and singing and laughter.

It's a powerful memory that makes me pause for a moment.

Then I reply with sincerity: 'Absolutely one hundred per cent not.'

16 December 1995 – LIAM

Day off.

End up in the pub, havin' a laugh, things starting to get a bit out of hand. Someone offers me a tab of acid.

'It's been a while,' I say. 'But go on then.'

'It's very strong,' says this bloke, so to show him, I take twice as much as he does.

Then someone's like: 'You know what would be fuckin' hilarious? Let's go to Noel's House Party.'

And I'm like, 'I didn't know he was having one?'

I thought he would of told me. But whatever, sure thing – only, by the time we get there the stuff is really kicking in. I'm finding it hard to concentrate and make out what's in front of me.

I'm introduced to a smug, self-important, bearded little gnome, and even though my vision's all distorted, I can tell it's him.

'Alright, Noel,' I say. 'What the fuck have you done with this place? It's mental!'

I'm just staring at the weird colourful walls and the tanks full of pink gunk, and wondering how much of it is true and how much in my mind, and how the fuck he's fit so many people into his house.

And then Noel says, 'I want to introduce you to a massive fan of yours. In fact he's had his own number one single . . .'

And through the door comes this fucking weird fucked-up giant marshmallow *Doctor Who* monster screaming and waving its arms. Somewhere in my brain I know it's not there, and that there's a real person inside that illusion.

But I can't control myself. I turn and run, and don't stop running until I'm shivering under a hedge by the side of an A road, as traffic swishes past. Clutching my knees. Wondering what part of my fucked-up brain that thing came out of.

12 January 1996 – LIAM

Fucking bullshit that Noel gets all the money from the song-writing, and the rest of us just get paid for performing. It can't be that hard banging out a few songs.

I reckon I could be the greatest songwriter in the world. Decided I'm gonna write some songs starting now. No one will even remember Noel when I'm done.

Spent an hour sitting there, trying to write. Was pretty tiring. Came up with this.

I saw that Patsy Kensit
I think she's really fit
Ooh yeah ooh yeah
La la la (reprise)

I saw that Patsy Kensit
I think she's ~~got really nice~~ would really get it
Ooh yeah ooh yeah
La la la (reprise)

Pretty knackered after that to be honest. Had a bit of a sleep. Good song though.

6 March 1996 – NOEL

Our drug dealer Baggsy, Billy the Bags, Bilbo Bag Ins, comes to us backstage.

'Ee up, fellers,' he says, as he's dishing the stuff out. 'Did I tell you about our new loyalty scheme? You get one of these cards, y'see – and each time you get a gram, you get a stamp. And once the card is full, you get a little . . . gratuity on the house, right?'

He's been focusing on counting out what he's delivering. Then he looks up and sees Noel and me both holding out fully filled-out loyalty cards.

'Ah,' he says, looking at them. 'I see today's business will be on the house . . .'

'Too right,' says Liam.

'When did I give you these?' he asks, tucking them into his pocket.

'Monday,' says Liam.

'Ah,' he says, withdrawing. 'Well then – merry Wednesday evening to you, lads!'

He turns back at the door. 'Don't suppose you fellers would be interested in our platinum service?'

'We're listenin',' I say.

THE GOSPEL ACCORDING TO LIAM

Being the Fifth Part

And so Oasis did go on tour in the Land of the Americans.

Now in this time, although the band were already big in England, they did not have any silver in their pockets. And to earn a few more shekels they did invest the per diems given them by the record label in a lot of Adidas trainers to sell to gullible American fans.

'And what the fuck shall we do with these?' askedeth Liam.

'Sell 'em out the back of the van for drug money,' said Bonehead.

'That going to work?' aksedeth Guigsy.

'Yeah, we can make like a three hundred per cent markup,' sayeth Bonehead.

For the band had so little spending money, that when they sold no tickets in Salt Lake City, Utah, in the Land of the Mormons, Noel did go out front of the venue and busk.

And he made only $1.84, which showeth you something about Utah. Or Noel's busking prowess. Or both.

And so they became both singers of songs and sellers of trainers.

During their time in the Land of the Americans they did have one gig in Vancouver, which was outside the Land of the Americans, in another place called Canada. And their tour manager came on the bus with a hoover and said unto them:

'You've got to clean this bus up from top to bottom because if the Canadian border sniffer dogs detect so much as a flipping whiff of drugs they will chuck you out, and the Americans won't let you back in, and then it's jail time and deportation.'

So they did bury their stash beneath an advertising hoarding off the highway, just by the American/Canadian border.

And they did succeed in getting through immigration and playing the gig, and travelling back.

And on coming to the spot beneath the advertising hoarding they did dig in the same spot, and lo, there was their stash unmolested by human, animal or weather. And they did reclaim it.

At which there was much rejoicing.

Truly it did seem Oasis were quickly becoming one of the biggest bands on the earth.

And the Gallagher brothers were taken by some promoters to a giant field in Hampshire. And in this place they were told they could do the biggest British gig of all time.

'We can sell a quarter of a million tickets,' said the promoters.

'But where will we perform?' asked Noel.

'Here,' said a promoter, carefully avoiding standing in a cowpat.

'But *where*?' Noel asked.

'This is a field. Where's the fucking stadium, you nipple?' asked Liam.

'We will build it here,' said the promoter. 'In this place that is called Knebworth.'

And the Gallaghers did look at the cows and trees all around, and wonder what the fuck they were talking about.

'Where would the stage be?' asked Noel.

'Over there,' said the promoter. 'Down that hill.'

'Over *there*?' asked Noel, pointing.

'No, the next hill after that,' said the promoter.

'How far away is that?' asked Liam.

'It's in Wiltshire,' admitted the first promoter.

'But we reckon we can sell out,' said the second promoter. 'For multiple nights. Maybe eight? But let's just start at two.'

And the Gallagher brothers did not know whether to laugh or to make a mess in their trousers.

Yet just as they doubted the words of the promoters, so it came to be.

For two and a half million of the people applied for tickets, which was unheard of.

On the night of Knebworth, the people came and crowded the fields across both counties, to listen to Liam.

And it was a great event, spoken of all across the land.

Even the television weather bulletin did advise about the specific weather for this gig, which when he saw it, Noel did think was some pretty wild shit.

When the time for the gig happened, Liam did appear in front of the host of people in a white parka, which did shine forth with great brightness.

Sorry, which did sheee-iiii-iiine forth with great brightness.

And he did play to a quarter of a million people just as the promoters had said, and he did see that it was good.

11 August 1996 – NOEL

A truly majestic experience, and something I will always be proud to have been a part of.

History was made this weekend.

A whole generation gathering to experience music and togetherness, a giant coming together of like-minded souls. A quarter of a million people united by music, by spirit, overcoming the difficulties of life in post-Thatcher Britain under the shitty Tory government. Roaring with happiness.

Rejecting the values we've been offered, making our own truth. Everyone who was there, part of the same collective spirit.

This was the most important musical event of our generation.

We made it happen.

I will never forget this.

I feel so proud.

11 August 1996 – LIAM

Did Knebworth gig.

Was good.

Apricots and yoghurt for breakfast.

Fucking love apricots.

Went back to bed and Marcus* woke me up, and I asked if the helicopter was ready to take us back.

* Marcus Russell, Oasis manager.

'You're joking right,' said Marcus. 'You've got a gig to do.'

'We done the gig last night, you flipping banana,' I said.

'Are you alright in the head?' he asked. 'It's two gigs, Liam.'

'Oh,' I said. 'Is that right? Alright then.'

So I did the second gig.

Went well.

Apricots for breakfast again next morning.

I fucking *love* apricots.

14 August 1996 – NOEL

Everyone in the music industry is suddenly talking about this new group which sounds like it was made for ten-year-old girls. We're all talking about it in the pub when Liam comes in.

Our Kid doesn't read papers, doesn't listen to the news.

Somehow this moron doesn't seem to have heard about the Spice Girls.

When we realise this, the rest of us spot a chance and don't miss a beat.

'You heard about Posh Spice, Liam – new expensive curry place in town?' Guigsy asks.

'Yeah,' he says.

'First curry chain in Britain run just by women,' I say.

'Fair play to 'em,' says Bonehead.

Liam nods like he knows all about it.

'I've not been,' I say. 'But I know they've got a van outside

Old Trafford and Maine Road selling onion bhajis and stuffed naans to footy fans. What's that one called?' I ask Guigsy.

'Sporty Spice,' says Bonehead. 'Apparently that's good too. That's right, innit Liam?'

'Yeah,' he says, after a slight hesitation. 'Yeah, I've heard it's OK. Yeah.'

'They've a place that does the hottest curry in Manchester,' says Tony.

'Scary Spice?' I say. 'Not been there yet.'

'I've been there,' says Liam, nodding and looking all-knowing. 'It's shit.'

Now everyone's interested. We all lean in.

'There's a hole-in-the-wall joint next to Scary Spice, just for takeaways,' I say. 'Tiny. Just one window. They call it Baby Spice.'

'Yeah, tried that an' all,' says Liam. 'Saag aloo was alright.'

'Liam, I'm impressed,' says Guigsy.

'Ahead of the game as always,' says Bonehead.

'Yeah,' says Liam complacently, leaning back and looking at us all down the length of his nose, through his shades.

'I fancy a curry,' I say. 'Ginger Spice is the nearest one. You order for me, Liam, yeah?'

'Yeah,' agree the others.

'I don't even know where it is,' says Bonehead. 'You go and order for us, right?'

'Right,' says Liam and, tenner in hand, wanders outside, no doubt stopping strangers in the street to ask them where he can eat out at Ginger Spice.

20 September 1996 – NOEL

There's a telly on in the corner of the room, with a documentary on, and Liam points at it.

'I don't get this shit, man. Like, evolution and that. Are you trying to tell me I'm related to a monkey? That's bullshit.'

'Liam,' I say. 'Evolution is just how living things slowly change and improve, over time. It's natural. It's kind of obvious once you see it.'

'Like what?' he asks.

'Well, like Oasis,' I say. 'First you've just got two lads, Guigsy and Bonehead. Rehearsing together on Friday nights. Then after a while they get Chris Hutton to sing, and a drum machine. And they're a band, right. And then, later on, they get a drummer, Tony McCarroll, and they rehearse some more. And then do some gigs. Right?'

He's nodding along. Frowning a bit, although this shouldn't be too hard for him to follow.

'But Chris sings flat and forgets the words so they fire him and hire this mouthy local nobhead called Liam.'

'And I'm not playing for a band called The Rain cos it's a dogshite name,' he says.

'Right. So the name gets changed to Oasis. And you rehearse and do gigs for ages. Then I join, and we get some new songs. Then we rehearse constantly for a year. The band is changing all the time. Then we start doing gigs proper, and after a while – bam. We get a deal, and Tony leaves, and then *Definitely Maybe* comes out. Right? We evolved slowly. Oasis wasn't just born overnight. That's evolution.'

'Yeah, whatever,' he says. 'Say what you like. But I'm still not related to monkeys and that's fucking that.'

And he walks away with his familiar swaying, bandy-legged walk, hooting at the top of his voice and eating a banana.

20 April 1997 – LIAM

Cigarettes: 76
Cans of lager: 15
White lines: 8
Saw a copy of that famous book, *Bridget Jones*, lying around. Had a look at it.

It's shit.

30 July 1997 – NOEL

Invited to Downing Street tonight for a champagne reception.

Me and McGee laughing all the way there in our Rolls-Royce, thinking about where we've come from. And where we've ended up.

Inside, Downing Street is surprisingly small. There was Cherie Blair, giving me the eye, and Peter Mandelson doing the most embarrassing dad-dancing in the world. But still. A politician, so what do you expect.

Press outside went mad when we arrived, asking McGee and me questions about whether we've betrayed our roots and our fans by coming to a champagne event held in the heart of the Establishment.

Anything that helps get the Tories out is OK by me. If we've helped New Labour, then quite frankly: you're welcome.

A bunch of famous folks milling around under the chandeliers. Glasses of champagne in hand. Talked to some, not to others.

Found myself looking at Tony Blair and Gordon Brown. Showy frontman who people think is basically quite shallow, and beside him the brains behind the whole outfit, less superficially attractive but the engine of their success.

Something slightly disturbing about this dynamic, but I can't quite put my finger on it.

4 August 1997 – NOEL

On tour.

Liam comes into my hotel room, bored.

There's something about him that annoys me today, more than usual. He's lounging around, doesn't know what to do.

He's already been for a walk round the local park three times. I want to get on with songwriting and he's mithering me.

'Been round the park three times you say?' I ask.

He nods, bored.

'So you've already been living your own park life,' I say.

'Yeah,' he says. 'Could say that.'

'You know what you could do,' I say. 'You're complaining about not having anywhere to live. You could look for a big house in the country.'

'But I want to live in the city.'

'Could have a *look* though. Nice big house in the country?'

'Nah.'

'Could be your great escape,' I say.

He's lying on the bed, looking out of the window.

'Everyone wants to get away somewhere. It's the universal,' I say.

'Nah,' he says.

'Alright then, suit yourself. Just have some coffee and TV, then.'

'Yeah,' he says. 'Good idea.' And he flips on the telly and calls room service.

It's like talking to someone with no brain.

Fuck it.

I give up.

It's the story of a charmless man.

LIAM GALLAGHER'S HISTORY OF BRITAIN

Episode 2: From the Normans to the Tudors

1348 – The Black Death

Everyone gets this horrible flu, but it's like worse than Covid.

Makes them get all blisters over their bodies and puke their guts up. Then they die screaming and with piss and pus streaming out of them.

Like imagine if everyone was forced to watch a Blur gig.

It's sort of like that.

Except maybe even a bit worse.

Because one in three people in Europe are killed in the space of five years.

Imagine if Blur had been around then, the casualties would probably have been even worse.

Although the band would have escaped because they'd have got away to their houses in the country to make cheese and have sound baths or some shit.

1455–87 – The Wars of the Roses

Different lads from York and from Lancaster are both like, 'I'm king, me – you can fuck right off.'

But basically they're all trying to pull a fast one, cos of their mums shagging around and that, and no one being sure who's dad's what or something. So whoever wins the ruck gets the headgear.

Except no one can win it proper and it goes on for like thirty years, which is longer than most people live in them days.

Anyway, some wanker called Henry finally wins it.

Dunno why it's called the Wars of the Roses. But family arguments do happen when the chocolates go round after Christmas dinner.

1509–47 – Henry VIII

He's a fine-looking feller, you've got to say. Looks dead pleased with himself.

But aside from that he's got everything wrong.

He's marrying women left, right and centre, in order to have *more* kids.

I've been there, and that's not the way to do it. Also, dickhead keeps beheading people. Which is not good karma.

Chops a few of his wives' heads off. You're not supposed to approve of such things these days, of course, though we all know it could be tempting at times. But I can't help feeling it's not the answer. Come on, Henry.

Just pick more carefully, you chubby idiot.

And stop standing there eating capons, no one even knows what they are. Call it TFC – Tudor Fried Chicken.

Sets up his own religion though, doesn't he. Cos he wants a divorce.

A religion which is still going strong, five hundred years later.

That's a head scratcher.

1588 – The Spanish Armada

Bunch of paella-munching Spaniards get in their boats (probably after a big afternoon nap) to invade England.

Except they go the wrong way round and get smashed up on the rocks.

Daft fuckheads.

Learn to sail a boat, mate. Stop eating gazpacho soup and get to learn how to use a boat like everyone else.

Maybe listen to the fucking shipping forecast. Translate it en espagnol.

They'd rather stay there and have fights with cows. Very impressive, Spaniards. We're quivering in our boots here. If they try and invade again we'll just give 'em some cows to fight.

c. 1600 – William Shakespeare and the Globe Theatre

OK, so they've only got like one theatre in the whole world at this point. And it's all people have got cos cinema's not been invented yet. But I'm guessing they can still get unlimited entries for like four farthings a month or something, like at Cineworld.

People back then are stuck watching all this boring wordy stuff by William Shakespeare because they've got like four hundred years until the *Fast and Furious* franchise is invented. Which starts good, then gets shit, but then gets good again despite the fact Vin Diesel's back in it, who is very obviously a total nobhead. And the fifth one is the best, but all after that are OK, even the one where they drive a car in space.

But back then they did have witches and murders and shit, so you've got to say, fair play, it wasn't all just talking like 'thee I havest knocked out a line for thou my maiden' and that.

Also it was like a proper gig because people shouted and threw vegetables and shit. And were even like shagging in the audience, and going toilet right there and then. Which is keeping it pretty real – like to see that Ian McKellen remember his lines if there was blowjobs and diarrhoea in the front row.

Know what I mean?

21 September 1997 – NOEL

Our Kid's birthday. What do you get for the loudmouth git who's already a millionaire?

What about for a loudmouth git who thinks he's reincarnated from John Lennon, even though John Lennon was still alive while he was alive, which makes zero fucking sense if you think about it for a moment even if you believe in the (pretty fucking stupid) idea of reincarnation anyway?

Long rhetorical question.

This Lennon thing started as a joke.

I saw it in his eyes as he said it, that he was just taking the piss. Maybe trying something on.

And then fame – success – a mountain of cocaine . . .

And now Our Kid claims to take it seriously.

So I've got him a trip to a medium to look into his past lives. Top-level stuff, a grand for an hour's visit. Guaranteed spectral visitation to former existences and all that.

For once, he's well chuffed with it, and off he goes to Madame Zyginsky or whatever she's called.

But I've got it all planned and organised just nice, haven't I? I've put in five extra notes for an extra-special reading, and rehearsed her good and proper at what she's got to do.

My instructions are strict. She's to get him under, and when he's hypnotised say she knows he used to be a musician in a former life. *You were famous all around the world*, she's going to say. *In fact I can even hear the music you are most famous for now. It's coming through the ether . . .* He's obviously tripping at this point, expecting to hear 'I Am the Walrus'.

And there's going to be a little record player behind a curtain, already running, with the greatest hits of George Formby ready to drop at this point.

He comes back later and his face is like thunder.

'How was it?' I ask, all innocent. 'You find anything out?'

He snarls at me not to ask.

'OK,' I say. 'Someone got out of the wrong side of the bed this morning. Tell you what, a thought popped into my head earlier. You've got a good nerve for heights, always did have. If the music stuff doesn't work out I reckon you could have a good career cleaning windows. You ever thought of that? It could suit you, you'd be good!'

Luckily I duck just quick enough to avoid the chair he's thrown.

10 March 1998 – LIAM

I'd never been to Australia before.

It's full of aggressive, shouting dickheads who are constantly up for a fight.

All they do is talk bollocks and drink all day long. Thicker than two short planks, most of them.

It's absolutely hotter than fuck.

You can hardly find a drink that isn't lager.

Feels like a home away from home, but less shit.

Fucking love it.

10 March 1998 – NOEL

Been on tour for eight months now.

Maddest shit we've ever done. Constant craziness.

Now we're in Australia for two weeks.

Should have been straightforward, but unfortunately Liam threatened to stab the pilot of the plane we flew here on.

This acting-aggressive shit got old quickly. Now it's been old for so long, its being old has got old.

First there was the fight on the way to Amsterdam. Stopped us playing our first big gig. Then the fuck-up at the Whiskey a Go Go.

Weird to say, but I'm starting to sympathise with Liam. He just says what he thinks. Why do they keep sticking a microphone under his nose?

You take one look at him, you know what you're getting. He's not complicated. He's a rock star. If he's bored, he'll say something aggressive.

Just stop asking his fucking opinion!

Questions now being asked in Australian parliament about whether we should get chucked out of the country. Maybe we should, I don't fucking care. Take me out of this dry, giant, ugly rock covered with poisonous spiders, snakes and racists. Even the fucking beer doesn't taste good.

And they don't serve it in pints.
Bunch of cunts.

28 April 1998 – NOEL

Arrive at a gig to find I've got a journalist waiting to interview me. Apparently I promised to do it – so I sit down in a pretty bad mood, and crack open a can of lager from our rider.

'Do you have any weird things in your rider?' asks the journo.

'One or two maybe,' I say. 'But that's private. You know, contractual stuff.'

'I get it,' he says. 'I was interviewing They Might Be Giants the other day.'

'They Might Be Soft Indie Ponces, you mean,' I say.

'We were talking about how acts put weird stuff in their riders – like Van Halen, who famously ordered a bowl of M&Ms with the brown ones taken out. You know what they said? It was interesting. They said with a big band, there's so much stuff to put in, so much complicated electronic stuff that can go wrong. If it's not been done properly, they could die. And the best way of checking that the venue has paid attention to the details is to ask for something like the M&M thing. Then you can see at a glance whether the gig has been properly set up.'

'That's interesting,' I admit.

'Kind of reassuring that no pop star would be so insane as to actually demand a bowl of M&Ms with the brown ones taken out, right? Just on a whim, I mean.'

'Agreed,' I say.

At that moment Liam walks in, and an assistant comes after him.

'Mr Gallagher,' she says. 'Here's the plate of milk chocolate Hobnobs with all the chocolate scraped off, as requested in your rider.'

'He's convinced the biscuit they use in the chocolate ones is nicer than in the plain ones,' I say.

'But I don't like the chocolate they put on 'em,' Liam says.

'And here's the two hundred B&H put into Silk Cut packets and resealed,' says the assistant, holding up a plastic bag.

'Patsy don't like me smoking B&H,' he says. 'She says they're bad for ya. Silk Cut's the healthy choice.'

And he's off out the door.

'Moving on,' says the journo.

25 February 1999 – LIAM

Went to a function tonight.

Who do I meet but the fucking Dalai Lama.

Tiny little feller, nearly as small as Noel. Wearing a stupid fucking red curtain.

He smiles up at me with his twinkling little eyes.

‘I have heard of you,’ he says, shaking my hand. ‘You are a musician.’

‘Course you have, mate,’ I say. ‘I’m the best fucking rock star on earth.’

‘For those who have been handsomely rewarded by life, humility can be healthy,’ he says.

‘I’m the humblest fucker on earth too, mate. Humblest you’ll ever meet.’

He nods and smiles again. Apparently that’s all he does in his life – goes around nodding and smiling and wearing curtains.

Everyone else in the room looks sort of shocked, and like they’re shitting themselves. So I think I’d better say something.

‘I’ve heard of you,’ I say. ‘You’re like the Indian pope or some shit.’

That stops him smiling for a moment. But only for a moment.

Then he nods and smiles again.

‘You’ve met George Harrison?’ I ask.

He nods. ‘Many times.’

‘Alright musician,’ I say. ‘But as a person I reckon he’s a nipple. Needs some more meat pies.’

‘The nipple is an important part of the human body,’ he says.

I hadn’t thought of that.

He's right.

Before I can think of anything to say back, he's fucked off.

Imagine being named after a llama though.

That would be like me being called Liam Gallagher Crocodile. Noel Gallagher Platypus.

Or some shit.

Actually, I wouldn't mind that.

22 June 1999 – NOEL

Tonight's gig was mega.

Relaxing after, with a drink and some friends.

Then a fan comes over and I get talking to them, but they've got a friend with them. And the friend suddenly pipes up and is like:

'Noel, aren't you now just a rich guy, with no contact with the lives of the people who you write songs for?'

It catches me unawares. I'm offended.

'I'm not saying you're a class traitor,' this girl says. 'But don't you think you've lost touch with your fans?'

I turn to Bono, who says, 'No way, Noel's just as real as he ever was.'

'That's right,' agrees Prince.

'Absolutely,' says Keith Richards.

Placido Domingo, taking a sip of champagne, nods in agreement.

'I stand corrected,' says the fan.

20 October 1999 – LIAM

'So what's this internet thing, then?' Noel asks, when he's round mine.

'You don't know what it is?' I say, looking up from my laptop.

'No,' he admits. 'Except it sounds geeky and annoying, but everyone keeps talking about it.'

'You're missing out,' I tell him. 'It's where people can talk about stuff that they like, and buy stuff. But fuck that, it's mostly about . . .' I angle my laptop towards him, and show him a few favourite websites.

'Can I borrow this for a minute?' he asks.

I'm not sure about that but I say, 'Yeah – just for a bit.' I pop down the road for some fags, but when I come back I can hear him groaning.

'Oi nobber,' I say, knocking on my own living room door. 'Am I safe to come in?'

'This is *amazing*,' he's saying. 'Wow! It's endless!'

'OK, that's enough,' I reply, coming in. 'Gimme it back.'

He's glued to the screen, can't take his eyes away.

'Listen to this,' he says. '"I genuinely think Noel Gallagher is the best songwriter in the world." Although they spelled "world" wrong, but that's alright. "Noel is a true genius and his songs mean so much to me." Here's another. "Undoubtedly the greatest musician of his generation." And listen to this . . .'

I close the door quietly and go off to the pub.

THE GOSPEL ACCORDING TO

LIAM

Being the Sixth Part

When Liam's fans were gathered in his presence, Liam spoke unto them.

And he did say: 'For was not my arrival foretold, by the coming of Ian Brown?'

And his fans did say: 'Well . . . not *partic*ularly.'

And he did say: 'Fuck you, it was an' all.'

And his fans did say: 'Alright. In a way, I suppose.'

And he did say: 'Fuckin' have it.'

'And am I not a reincarnation of the great prophet John Lennon?' he askedeth them at a later date, in a rhetorical fashion.

The fans did not really see that he was. But they did love Liam and so they did not openly argue that Liam had been alive for many years while John Lennon was still alive, so the concept that he was a literal reincarnation was reckoned to be obvious bullshit even if reincarnation could possibly be true, which soundeth like wishful thinking at best.

Unless you were a Buddhist or some shit.

As Liam went among the peoples of the earth, spreading his message, he did find himself among the people of Munich.

Which was the place where Noel had phoned Peggy from to hear about the band in the first place, as it happens, for ye fans of ye facts.

And Liam did refresh himself in a common tavern, as was his wont for he was one of the people. And did never turneth up his nose at a pint or six of lager when he had a few hours to kill, even if he had to sit in a room of Germans.

There being much time until his gig was to begin, Liam did spot some strangers at the bar who from their speech he took to be Italian tourists.

And the spirit of boredom being upon him, he did flick peanuts at them.

And when they did notice and turn to look at him, he did taunt them. And ask them if they wanted to have it.

Liam's disciples being around him, and the spirit of boredom being upon them also as with him, did join in this question. And they did join in a fight with the Italians.

Yet his sight did betray him, for these were no tourists, but were members of the mafia, who were Most Displeased to be treated with disrespect.

And so they took to fighting.

And the members and roadies of Oasis did discover that while getting in a ruck with some fans of another band or a football team in Glasgow or Liverpool or Millwall was quite an entertaining pastime, fighting professional organised criminals was considerably less amusing.

And Liam did have a bunch of his teeth kicked out.

And it may be surmised that on this day he perhaps learnedeth a lesson.

Or on reflection maybe not.

31 December 1999 – NOEL

Big millennium party, lots of famous faces.

Then I spot Our Kid and wave to him.

'I've got a word to have with you,' he says. 'Listen, I've had it with people thinking I'm gullible, right?'

'Who says that?' I ask.

'Fuck off, man, you're always taking the piss. I don't, like, read books and shit like you, but I'm not stupid.'

'Liam, like many people, you are very intelligent in some ways,' I shout over the noise of the party. 'And not so much in others. Right?'

As it happens, I am being sincere. I think he sees this.

'Alright,' he says. 'I just don't like you putting it about that I fall for stupid tricks all the time, OK? Cos I don't know shit like you do. It winds me up.'

I give him a straight look and nod. Punch him on the shoulder.

'Good to be at the party with you, buddy,' I say. 'Gonna be a big one. The millennium! By the way, you prepared for the Y2K bug?'

'Yeah,' he says, and holds his jacket open so I can see into his pocket. 'Got Lemsip and Beechams, just like you said. I'm ready!'

'Good lad,' I say. 'The bug's going to be everywhere at midnight. Don't want to get caught out.'

'Glad you warned me,' he says. 'You're not a total cunt all the time.'

'That I'm not,' I say.

22 July 2000 – NOEL

Worst professional experience of my life – two nights at Wembley.

Liam acts up, gets the words of the songs wrong, insults the crowd for being there.

This is being filmed for a live DVD.

Everything's falling apart. But then gradually I find out it's because Patsy left him the night before the big gig. She's taken everything, emptied out his house.

'She didn't even leave me a fucking teabag,' he says. Live, to 77,000 people. And millions of TV viewers.

I once got in trouble in the press for saying taking drugs is just as normal as having a cup of tea.

Now Our Kid hasn't even got a teabag, and his wife has done a bunk. It's pretty understandable that he's had a line or two.

That's when I realise that for him right now, doing drugs is *more* normal than having a cup of tea.

27 July 2000 – LIAM

Outside a party after a long night, smoking a blunt, and this fit bird walks over. I know her.

And suddenly I realise, I've fancied her for ages, and we've met before. And I've seen her on telly and that.

Got a feeling I don't want to fuck this up – birds don't like it if you don't remember where you know them from.

Now, I was at a party last week with this magician feller Derren Brown, and he was telling me a way to remember shit. Except I can't remember what he said. I'm racking my brains. For his advice, and for her name.

So I'm nodding and chatting to her, right, and piecing it together. She's in a band. And I'm thinking of what it reminds me of . . . And for some reason I'm thinking of that clothes shop. Then I have like a light bulb moment.

'You're that fit bird from All Souls,' I say.

'All Saints,' she says.

'Yeah right, 'swhat I said. You see, I remember cos of when I first met you, it was outside that church, right. All Souls. That's beside that clothes shop.'

'All Saints,' she says.

'Nah,' I say. 'Think it was River Island.'

'Never mind,' she says, smiling. 'I'm Nicole. I can't forget your band name because the first time we met, we ended up going to a kebab shop at five a.m. that was called Oasis.'

'Oh yeah?' I say. 'I mean – yeah, I remember.'

'And I got salmonella *and* ringworm. So whenever I see you I think of vomiting uncontrollably, and I remember – Oasis!'

'Nice one,' I say.

I like this bird.

13 July 2004 – LIAM

Haven't been to the cinema for donkey's years. Want to get out of the house.

Nicole fancies *Shrek 2*. I want to watch *Spider-Man 2*.

Both sold-out. Only tickets left are for *Downfall*.

Nicole's up for it.

'Tell me what it's about then,' I say.

She tells me it's about the last few days of Hitler's life, going mad in his bunker.

I think about it.

'Two tickets for *Downfall*, then?' asks the kid behind the counter. He looks over my shoulder where there's a queue forming.

'Nah,' I say. 'I don't want to watch a film about a self-important grumpy short-arsed tyrant who thinks he ought to be charge, having a mental breakdown and making everyone miserable. Movies are supposed to be about escaping from everyday life.'

'He's talking about Noel,' says Nicole.

'Yeah, I got it,' says the ticket seller. 'Very amusing.'

'It was actually quite clever. You're really clever, darling.'

'Thanks, babe. You're really fit.' And she gives me a big snog.

'Next please,' says the ticket seller.

28 August 2009 – LIAM

****** Noel *** ** *** ***** ** ***!

He ****** *** ***** **** * **** *****!!! ***** *** ** *** **** ***** *** **** **** ***. ***** *** **** *** ** * ****** *** *** *** **** * ***** **** *** * **** ****** **** **** *** guitar **** **** ****** ** *** *** ***** **** **** *** * * ** *** *** *** *** Noel ** ***** ****** *** *** * ***** ******* ****** **** *** ***** ***** ** * ***** * **** **** ***.

*** ** ****** *** ** *** *** *** ** *** * stupid **** ***.

**** ** *** **** *** ***** ******* ***** **** *** * **** ***** ***** **** *** **** ** **** ** ** *** ******.

*** ***** *** ** Oasis ***** **** **** **** **** ******* **** ***** **** ******* ****** ***** **** *** **** *** **** **** ***** ** Noel ** *** ** ***** **** ** **** *** **** *** *** **** *** ** * * ** *** *** **** **** **** ** *** *** **** ***** *** **** *** **** ****.

28 August 2009 – NOEL

Liam ****** *** ** dumb *** ***** ** ***!

****** *** ***** **** * **** *****guitar ***** *** ** *** **** ***** *** **** **** ***. ***** *** **** *** ** * ****** *** *** *** **** * ***** **** *** * **** ****** **** **** *** everywhere **** **** ****** ** *** *** ***** go back **** **** *** * * ** *** *** *** *** ** ***** ****** *** **** ***** ******* ****** **** *** ***** ***** ** * ***** * **** **** ***.

*** ** Liam ****** *** ** *** *** *** ** *** * and **** ***.

**** ** *** **** *** ***** ******* ***** **** *** * **** ***** ***** **** *** **** ** **** ** ** *** ******.

*** ***** *** Liam ** ***** **** **** **** **** ******* **** ***** **** ******* ****** ***** **** *** **** *** **** **** ***** ** ** *** ** ***** **** ** **** *** **** *** *** **** *** ** * * ** *** *** **** **** **** ** *** *** **** ***** *** **** Oasis *** **** **** *forever!*

OTHER OASIS DOCUMENTS

Along with the diary entries, the Gospel and Liam Gallagher's History of Britain, certain other documents were discovered in the cache which seem to be a somewhat random collection of secret business dealings and correspondence.

They appear to date from various periods during the early years of Oasis's success and their reunion. They are gathered here together in the following pages – after which the diaries resume.

S.P. (Editor)

MEMORANDUM:

AD CAMPAIGNS REJECTED BY NOEL GALLAGHER

1994: LEVI'S JEANS [Offer withdrawn after all samples sold on Manchester market stall]

1995: OAKLEY SUNGLASSES [Offer withdrawn after all samples smashed by Liam Gallagher 'in like a total accident mate sorry']

1996: NEW LEATHER JACKET RANGE BY ARMANI [Rejected – girlfriend objects to leather]

1997: MITSUBISHI MOTORBIKE [Rejected – can't drive]

2024: NU-COMFORT BRAND MEN'S INCONTINENCE PADS [Rejected but samples accepted with thanks]

2025: MEDDLINGTON'S WALK-IN BATHS [Rejected with handwritten note: 'Fuck you I'm not that old yet']

2025: BRILLIANZ HAIR PRODUCTS 'RETHICKEN YOUR THATCH' HAIR COLOUR RANGE [Rejected with polite note saying Oasis management has been ordered to stop accepting pitches for advertising campaigns as 'Mr Gallagher finds them distressing at this time']

REJECTED OASIS MERCHANDISE

Oasis Top Trumps

Enjoy BATTLING the different members of your favourite Band in an endlessly entertaining card game for ~~all ages~~ **older players only**!

PIT current and former members of the band OASIS – as well as other players in the Oasis story – against each other. WHO WILL WIN?

Each playing card represents a person who played a crucial role in the band's formation, their fame, their downfall or their resurrection!

Every character is awarded a score based on six different criteria:

Having It:	⋆ to ⋆⋆⋆⋆⋆
Durability:	⋆ to ⋆⋆⋆⋆⋆
Moolah:	⋆ to ⋆⋆⋆⋆⋆
Tabloid Coverage:	⋆ to ⋆⋆⋆⋆⋆
Mancunianocity:	⋆ to ⋆⋆⋆⋆⋆
White Lines:	⋆ to ⋆⋆⋆⋆⋆

Tony McCarroll scores 5⋆ for Mancunianocity and White Lines, but scores low for Durability. Damon Albarn gets a high score for Tabloid Coverage and Moolah, but zero for his Mancunian credentials. Alan McGee appears as two different cards, one for his (White Lines heavy) pre-1994 self, and a second after he got clean, but sold Creation to Sony for a seven-figure sum, making this version of him a 5⋆ Moolah card, as well as scoring high on Tabloid Coverage for his 1997 visit to Downing Street.

Oasis – The Video Game (1994)

A side-scrolling action arcade beat-'em-up game where players play as Liam or Noel.

Each level is a different environment. BONUSES are achieved by kicking or smashing dustbins, which will then release bags of COCAINE (which give a Strength bonus) or TRAINERS (a Speed bonus). Cars can also be beaten until they catch fire and explode, killing any characters who are nearby.

Level One: The backstreets of Manchester. The Gallaghers have to defend themselves against street thugs, social workers and police. Liam is armed with a pool cue, Noel with a Gibson Les Paul guitar.

Level Two: Within the corridors of an Evil Record Company, the Gallaghers have to defeat the rapacious SECRETARIES and EXECUTIVES who wield vicious sharpened pens, and PAPARAZZI who temporarily disable the players with their bright flashing cameras.

They fight their way to the BOARDROOM, where the mutated alien-like head of the company is trying to force them to sign an UNFAIR CONTRACT in their own blood. Once they defeat this beast they are rewarded with multiple permanent STRONG COCAINE AND ULTRA SNEAKERS power-ups and improved PARKA 'skins'/costumes that grant them extra Stamina and allow them to withstand attacks.

Level Three: [Most arcade players will not reach this level – it requires multiple dozens of fifty-pence plays to reach this stage.] The Gallaghers travel through a PARKLIFE level, surviving insane joggers and people walking their HOUNDS to go up against BLUR at a COUNTRY HOUSE final boss fight.

Oasis Children's Books

Dear Mr Gallagher,

It was most interesting to meet with you earlier this week at our offices to discuss a potential series of new children's books. As I said at the time, I am committed to bringing entertaining books to young working-class male readers, who are sorely underserved in the current market. This letter is a memorandum of what we discussed.

I had pitched to you a series of adventures of ***Liam and his Bandmates****, aimed at the 6–8-year-old age range, in settings that our readers will feel comfortable with. In the sample story I showed you, Liam has lost his football and goes searching for it.*

First he looks in the underprivileged inner-city school (most attractively decorated with graffiti), then at the Job Centre, next at a bookmaker's (Ladbrokes, for instance), where he is cheered on by the friendly toothless denizens. At last he finds his dear football at the park, which is prettily lit by flames from a tyre conflagration.

At each of these locations he discovers one of his friends, the smiling children who are his future bandmates in Oasis. And in happiness at the end they play a song together on little instruments.

Your opinions about this story idea were forthright and colourful. (One might almost think that you were 'refreshed', were it not ten o'clock in the morning, ha ha!)

You offered your own story ideas, which were that Liam eats a 'special mushroom' that turns him into a giant crocodile which sneezes acid, and fights a giant Russian robot before sticking some dynamite – I think I misheard the next bit, but it involved Margaret Thatcher, and ended with her exploding. You added most characteristically that he should be 'well buff' and get with a girlfriend crocodile 'who's all fit like, like you know the way they make rabbits sexy in them Warner Brothers cartoons'.

I do not think we have either of us quite cracked the storyline yet, but I would be pleased to be in touch in future to discuss this project further. ('And as I mentioned, I would be most delighted if you happened to have spare concert tickets for my niece Victoria.)

Yours sincerely,
Emma Patherington-Smedhurst,
Editorial Director, Little House Books

OASIS CONTRACTUAL RIDER FOR CARDIFF, 5 JULY 2025

TO BE READY ON ARRIVAL:

2 rosemary-scented neck pillows (Harrods)

4 packets of Himalayan camomile tea (Fortnum's brand)

Masseur (minimum height 5′, maximum height 5′6″) to offer rubdown at half-hour intervals

TV (minimum 62″) with subscription to UK history and gardening programmes and tested batteries in controllers

Rice cakes (unflavoured) x 24

Racing Post (current edition)

OASIS DIARIES – THE REUNION

1 February 2024 – LIAM

Doing interviews all day.

'Don't say nothing rude,' says Debbie.* In the old days I wouldn't have let a publicist talk to me that way, but she's also me bird, like.

So thanks to her I'm slowly getting a bit better at not blowing up at journos.

Just to keep things quiet at home like.

But this slimy journo prick gets one in at me just at the end.

'Your fashion brand, Pretty Green, was rescued from administration in 2019,' he says. 'If your brother had a fashion brand, what do you think it would be called?'

'I dunno,' I say. 'Shitty Brown?'

'Don't print that,' says Debbie.

'Listen to her, she's in charge,' I say. 'Why don't you just save yourself time and ask her the questions? Like why she puts up with me anyway?'

'Oh, I know the answer to that,' the journo says.

'Oh yeah? What do you mean?'

'Well,' he says, smiling at Debbie. 'She already did the second most difficult job in rock, which was being your

* Debbie Gwyther.

publicist. And having realised she could do that, she decided to take on the *most* difficult one, which is being your other half.'

Debbie nearly smiles, I can see.

Prick.

10 February 2024 – LIAM

Heard on the news that even though Covid's died down, there's a chance there could be another pandemic at any time.

Maybe worse than the last one.

Fuck that, mate.

All those months mooching around the house, not going out, not talking to people.

Feeling like some kind of demented ferret, a pointless goon who nobody likes. And no one wants to talk to. Just stuck on my own writing sad fucking songs about being miserable.

Can't go through that again.

Might as well be Noel.

2 March 2024 – NOEL

Must've eaten some cheese before bed last night, or something.

Got to sleep before twelve.

Next thing I'm dreaming in the middle of a dark studio, with a spotlight on me. There's that annoying ponce in a desk opposite me.

'Noel, your specialist subject is Liam Gallagher, and your two minutes start now.'

'What?'

Then he starts firing questions at me.

I'm too startled to do anything but answer them.

And yeah, I know the cocky bastard better than anyone, cos he's my brother, right? My sense of competitiveness is too strong for me to get a question wrong, if I know the answer. Question, answer, question, answer, quickfire. A buzz every time I get one right. Then he's congratulating me and the audience is clapping respectfully.

I wake up sweating. Walk around the room, wondering what that was all about.

Finally get back to sleep around three.

Next thing, what do you fucking know but I'm in the *Mastermind* studio again.

But this time I'm in the audience.

Liam's there in the chair. Sprawled out, smoking a joint. Scratching his balls.

'Mr Liam Gallagher, your specialist subject is Pot Noodles – and nice shirt by the way – your two minutes start now . . .'

Before I know what's what, the audience is laughing their heads off at whatever he's said, and cheering like it's Knebworth.

I can hear his answers are all wrong, but he gets the world record for correct answers for some reason. The question master offers him a silver platter covered with cocaine and a rolled-up £1 million note. Then the audience are screaming, all the women have taken their tops off, and Liam's laughing his head off as they gather round him.

I wake up sweating even worse than before.

This afternoon my therapist told me I must have unresolved anxiety about my talented younger brother.

I told him to stop making stupid suggestions if he wants paying.

Wonder what it does mean though.

14 March 2024 – LIAM

Get in your fifties, you start to worry you're getting old. Can't remember why you went in a room. Have to try and get used to modern stuff and loads of shit you aren't used to.

I'm struggling with something when I hear some sounds downstairs. From the sound of it, the kids are visiting with some of their friends, so I go down.

'Hey, listen up, I need your help,' I say.

I'm kind of embarrassed at first, not sure how to ask.

'Look,' I say. 'It's this tablet. I just don't know how to work it.'

'Oh, that's all right. Just give it here,' one of my kids' friends says. 'It's dead easy, you'll get the hang of it in no time. Hand it over.'

'Right,' I say, offering it.

'You just put a twenty-pound note over it, crush it like this with a credit card, sort it into lines and then – you know what to do!' He offers the note.

'Right, right,' I say, rolling the note up.

'What's the tablet for?' he asks.

'For me fookin' angina. I've never been good at swallowing those things. This way's easy . . .'

16 March 2024 – LIAM

Phone rings.

'Now, Liam,' says an Irish voice. 'It's your mother.'

'Hello, my darlin',' I say. 'How can I help you this beautiful mornin'?'

'It's this tablet,' she says. 'I'll be damned if I can get the thing to work. I'm at sixes and sevens. You know how I am with modern things.'

'You've come to the right feller,' I say. 'Now you just listen to me . . .'

3 April 2024 – NOEL

Phone buzzes. It's Liam. I'm in the kitchen on my own.

Pick up the phone and just look at it buzzing for a moment.

'Well, would you fucking look at that,' I say. I put it down and let it buzz itself halfway across the table. Guess I'm wondering what to think.

Then, out of curiosity, I pick up.

Could be a prank, after all. What if some teenager found his phone in a hedge and thinks this is the funniest thing he could do with it. Let's say.

'Noel Gallagher speaking,' I say.

'Ey up,' he says.

It is him.

I look at the phone again. Fair play. I listen.

'You ever been offered a hundred and fifty million quid?' he asks.

'Now you mention it, no, I have not,' I say.

'Me neither,' he says.

'Right,' I say. 'How interesting. Well, do think of phoning another time to discuss important matters of the day . . .'

'I've been offered *two* hundred mill though,' he says. 'And now so have you.'

There's something arresting about the phrase 'two hundred mill'.

I have to let it go round my head for a bit, like a mouthful of proper expensive wine. The sort you normally only get poured when you're at Johnny Depp's house.

'Hello?' he asks.

'Yeah sorry,' I say. 'I was thinking.'

'I know. Doesn't happen every day.'

'What, me thinking?'

'The two-hundred-million-quid thing.'

'It does not,' I agree. 'You are right there.'

No one says anything for a moment.

'So, uh, what do you think?'

'It's a *lot* of money,' I say.

'That's what I was thinking,' he says. And hangs up.

I put the phone down on the kitchen table carefully, like it might explode.

So I suppose I'm in Oasis again.

THE GOSPEL ACCORDING TO
LIAM

Being the Seventh Part

A sad day did come when a fight between the brothers caused Oasis to split.

The split seemed absolute and irrevocable.

For when two brothers sincerely think the other is a fucking twat, nothing can repair the break, unless both change their minds.

Even when a thousand journalists ask questions of both brothers as to how a reunion might possibly occur, at every opportunity. And even create fake front-page news that a reunion is imminent. Which did occur like a whole bunch of times and did piss everyone off.

But on the day of the split a Holy Fire did appear and fill the hearts of the fans of Oasis.

And the spirit entered them, and they did not stop plaguing Noel Gallagher about a reunion for fifteen fucking years, day and night.

And he did say we will never reunite.

Like about fifty million times.

And then he did say, 'Look, all Our Kid has to do is ring me. But he never will.'

And he did continue to deny Oasis wouldst ever get back together despite also openly admitting he had a full stadium rock album written and ready to record, but that High Flying Birds was not the band to record it with.

Sorry, that *Noel Gallagher's* High Flying Birds was not the band to record it with.

So, many in the land were thinking unto themselves, OK mate, so what's your point?

And Liam did put out a lot of cryptic tweets which did make people wonder. And did generate work for clickbait 'journalists'.

But then Noel did sadly have a divorce.

And fans did note that Noel's ex-wife had described Liam as some kind of revolting illiterate scumbag.

And therefore, it was considered one did not have to be Sherlock Holmes to guess that Noel's wife had been one of the sticking points between them.

And also that Noel didst therefore have quite a lot fewer readies than he had heretofore been having had.

And at last it was announced there would be a reunion in the Year of Our LORD 2025.

And the fans of Liam did fall at his feet and say, the rebirth we were promised is upon us, and did send crying emojis, and did say, yay!!!! Fuckin have it lads!!!! etc.

And they did see this news as though it was veritably the Second Coming.

Excepteth that that already be the title of a Stone Roses album.

And much speculation there was, that they had recorded an album in secret at Liam's house in France.

This is the word of the LORD.

Amen.

Fuckin' 'ave it!

22 September 2024 – LIAM

Being in a rock band used to be all drugs and music.

Now it's all fucking meetings with people with long fucking job descriptions. It's cos there's more money involved, sure, but does money make up for being fucking bored?

Only half, I reckon.

Today's meeting is with Johnny, our business manager. He's got a hundred things for us to answer, in preparation for the reunion.

I'm snoozing through the lot of it.

'Now,' he says after about an hour. 'We got to talk seriously about plugs.'

That wakes me up.

'No way,' I say. Partly cos I've not said fuck all so far and I want to make it look like I was listening to the other shit. 'No fucking way. I've never plugged stuff on stage before and I won't now. You've changed, man. You never would of suggested this in the old days. You've changed. I'm insulted you've even suggested it.'

'No, Liam,' he says. 'I mean ear plugs. Your audience is not getting any younger. For insurance purposes, it's probably a very good idea if we give them out free at the gates. Don't want to send half of them deaf and give the other half tinnitus, then find ourselves on the business end of a class action lawsuit.'

‘Oh right,’ I say. ‘Yeah, whatever.’ I turn to Noel. ‘What do you think?’

‘What?’ he says. Then he fiddles with his ears, takes two little things out of them. ‘Hey, these really work. I couldn’t hear a thing. What have you two been mithering about for the last hour?’

‘Give me some of those,’ I say.

20 October 2024 – LIAM

We’re in a pub and Noel and a few of the others are talking about the American election.

Someone’s like, ‘What do you think, Liam?’

Noel just shakes his head. ‘Don’t ask him, he’s not interested.’

I hate it when he talks about me like I’m thick. Winds me right up. I could be interested in American politics, what does he know?

I mean, I’m not. But I could be. So I go: ‘That Trump bloke right, what a wanker. He’s off his head. No way he’ll get in again.’

‘And why’s that?’ asks Noel.

‘He’s a fuckin’ loony, mate,’ I say. ‘He lies all the time. He doesn’t even know what the truth is. And cheatin’ at golf and that – it’s pathetic.’

‘But we played golf at Alan McGee’s stag weekend, remember?’

'Yeah,' I say.

'And you cheated then.'

'That's different, I didn't know how the scoring worked.'

'I'll say you didn't,' says Noel. 'Despite me showing you how it worked, and explaining it in words of one syllable. Pretty simple: you write down the actual number of shots that you play.'

'Yeah, but I was unlucky,' I say. 'It was unfair. So I put down the number of shots I should of taken if it were fair.'

'Thinks he's Kim Jong Il,' says Noel to the others. 'Got two holes in one, in a row.'

'Nah, but seriously,' I say, not wanting to start the golf shit up again. 'Trump actually thinks he's the cleverest person in the world and anyone that argues with him should be dead. It's insane, right?'

'Excuse me,' says a voice, and we turn and there's this fan there.

We take a picture and then he asks me: 'Is it true you think you're the reincarnation of John Lennon?'

'Yeah, it's the truest thing in the fucking cosmos, mate,' I say. 'In fact I'm better than him, because I'm him reincarnated *and* I'm me, you see?'

'And he reckons he could run the whole world,' says Noel.

I think about that for a second.

'You know what, I *could* run the world!' I say. 'And I'd be the best bastard at it there's ever been. And anyone who disagrees with that wants stabbing, you know?'

'You'd win if you stood in an election?'

'Yeah.'

'And if you didn't win, the election was probably rigged, right?'

I think about that. It makes sense.

'Probably, yeah,' I say.

The fan gets me to sign an autograph, and while I'm doing it I see the others are all laughing for some reason.

Nobheads.

21 December 2024 – LIAM

In the nineties we just turned up at stadiums, played. Bit of nosebag before we went on, lots after.

Fucking simple.

Now everyone's shitting their pants that Our Kid and me are going to fight. Punch each other out. Or drop dead. That the big gigs will never happen.

All of a sudden I've got to do a dozen tests every ten fookin' seconds. Every time I turn around there's some cunt with a clipboard and a thermometer he's trying to stick up my arse.

Got sent for me physical last week.

So I go in there, and there's an eye test, with letters getting smaller the further you go down the chart.

'Read that for me, please, Mr Gallagher,' says this nobhead in a white coat.

'Easy,' I say. 'B, O, L, L, O, C, K, S.'

He's looking at his chart and he frowns and stuff, and peers into my eyes with his laser or whatever. He does not seem to have a sense of humour and I'm not explaining shit to him.

Have to admit I have had sort of this approach for most of the tests what I've had to take.

'Mr Gallagher, tell me how many cigarettes you've smoked today.'

'Like, fucking ninety or some shit.'

'Ninety?' He looks up at me.

'Yeah,' I say. 'Maybe more.'

He looks at the clock, it's ten thirty.

'And have you used any recreational drugs this week?'

'Course I have, mate. I'm a fucking rock star!' I turn to this nurse who's on the other side of the room and ask her: 'Who does this prick think he's talking to? I'm Liam fuckin' Gallagher!'

She just looks down, very embarrassed.

The posh-voiced white coat dickhead asks me to go into more detail.

I invent what I want to sound like an average weekend round me gaff. After a while I get into it, and end up describing some hedo-fuckin'-nistic shit. Sounds like Keith Richards's stag-do.

I can see it's making his eyes pop.

Later in the day my phone rings.

It's Noel. 'What did you say to that doctor, you nobhead?' he asks.

'Good morning to you too, Noel. He asked questions and I answered them.'

'What did you say exactly?'

I give him a slightly edited version.

'Jesus Christ! You made a weekend with you sound like a year with Jerry Garcia.' He pauses. 'Wait a minute. I saw you last weekend, you were fit as a fiddle. You were just back from the swimming pool – you're practically a fitness freak these days. Please don't tell me you made it up to impress the doctor.'

'Don't be stupid, of course I didn't,' I say.

'Some pretty nurse then,' he says.

I say nothing.

He sighs.

'I've got a reputation to maintain, ain't I, Noel?'

'Well, thanks to your reputation we can't get insured for these gigs. No insurance, no gig. You're going to have to do another physical, and actually be honest this time. Do it properly.'

'I was doing it properly!' I say. 'They were the answers a rock god ought to give.'

'*Properly* properly,' he says.

'I'll think about it,' I say.

Two days later I'm in a different doctor's office. Another posh prick.

'Tell me, Mr Gallagher, do you take any exercise?'

'Oh yeah,' I say. 'I go snowboarding, rock climbing, pretty regular like. Then I do parkour three times a week. And of course there's the Thai kickboxing as well.'

He nods, writing this down. 'Very impressi—'

'Karate, judo, jiu-jitsu, aikido, taekwondo and krav maga,' I say. 'You want me to go slower, so you can write all this down?'

I leave the office pleased with myself. A job well done. No fit nurses this time, though.

Rock-god reputation intact. And at least Noel can't have a problem with that.

My phone rings half an hour later.

'Liam! What the fuck!'

'You're going to have to work on your greetings, my brother. How can I help you?'

'What the hell did you tell *this* doctor?'

I tell him. Seems pretty reasonable to me.

'But Jesus, Liam, you're fifty-two years old. No one can do all that exercise full stop, especially not someone who's your age and has taken a skip's worth of cocaine in his time.'

'So what? Who cares?'

'Liam, they've turned us down for insurance again.'

'That's bullshit, man! I made myself sound like the healthiest person alive!'

'No, you didn't. You made yourself sound like a man who's a) insane, b) having some sort of mental breakdown and c) about to break his neck or his arm or his legs at any minute and call off the gigs. No one's going to insure that.'

'Why are we talking about insurance the whole time?'

'Cos we're not playing at the Boardwalk in Manchester, you fucking nobhead, these are ten-million-pound gigs! Come round mine right now . . .'

When I get there he's got the forms and is filling them out himself. 'OK. How many fags you smoked this week?'

'Well, none, actually,' I admit.

'How may units of alcohol you drunk?'

'Er,' I say, thinking about it. 'Now you mention it. None.'

Only takes five minutes to get the right answers out of him – the truth, as it happens, was all that was required, once I'd realised all I had to do was swallow my pride.

LIAM GALLAGHER'S HISTORY OF BRITAIN

Episode 3: From the Gunpowder Plot to the Battle of Waterloo

1605 – The Gunpowder Plot

Who doesn't like a fucking firework now and then. Am I right?

And also who doesn't hate politicians.

So some geezer tries to combine the two and make for the biggest fireworks display of all time. Absolute 100 per cent banger of an idea. Literally.

Unfortunately, the bloke who sold him the gunpowder, or maybe someone else, dobs him in.

Also when they catch him with like thirty-six barrels of gunpowder and some matches and they say, are you Guy Fawkes, he says no.

So what are you called, mate? they ask. Er, John Johnson, he says.

Less impressive. You've got to be able to think on your feet, Guy Fawkes mate.

So, they torture him up, poor bastard.

But he gives the world Fireworks Night, right, so he's got to be pleased with that. Win some lose some.

1649–1660 – Oliver Cromwell and the Interregnum

So in 1649 this Oliver Cromwell feller had Charles I's head chopped off, which everyone was like – yeah do it.

And then when they saw how well Chucky boy took it (cos he wore an extra shirt to stop him shivering), they were all like, oh fuck. We've shat the bed on this one.

Too right they had.

So Cromwell comes in and says – shit's going to change round here. He bans Christmas, and dancing, and music, and hangs people for like wearing nice clothes and smiling and stuff. No one wears make-up and they all have to walk round wearing like sacks.

So I'm guessing there's absolutely no shagging going on and the population's about to drop off a cliff. Let people wear a bit of lippy, Cromwell son, at least.

Banning music, man – what is this nobhead thinking? But then, the music in those days was bound to be shite, so maybe he's got a point. When you think about it you can sort of see both sides of the argument.

Anyway, then he dies and things move on pronto. The throne goes to Charles II, who has amazing hair like Brian May. He just comes in the door and is like: guys, it's party time. And Christmas and music and dancing and all that are back on. Imagine it.

Everyone must have wanted to give him one, no wonder the lad had syphilis.

1666 – The Great Fire of London

Some dickhead leaves the oven on.

Whole fucking place goes up. Guessing he burns the toast as well.

What a nobhead.

St Paul's Cathedral, loads of important places and nice pubs. Basically everyone's homeless.

But then it's London, so it was probably quite funny as well, to some folk at least.

It also wiped out the plague that had been killing thousands in London at the time.

Imagine if Blur were around, it probably would have wiped them out as well.

Nerdy twats.

Probably would have been too busy making pictures of the fire and then would have been burned inside Ye Olde Arte School.

1776 – The American War of Independence

Bunch of American farmer sheep-fuckers get up themselves that they have to pay tax. I haven't really looked into it but they may or may not have had a point.

Anyway, they decide to turn Boston harbour into the world's worst cup of cold-brew tea.

In life there are lots of situations which need to be looked at from different angles to get a true sense of what's right or wrong. However, let's get a sense of perspective for one second.

Up until this moment the Americans were British citizens, right?

Some things are sacred. And a cup of fucking tea is one of them.

So they're welcome to fuck off, quite frankly. Invent America and Starbucks and all the quadruple Big Mac and pumpkin spiced lattes and shit.

1815 – Battle of Waterloo

Napoleon's severely asking for it.

He's been taught a lesson and told to fuck off to his Mediterranean island, which is not a bad retirement plan.

Maybe one I'd consider myself.

But maybe they've run out of garlic toothpaste or something because he comes back giving it all that, hello, saying he's going to start the war again.

So Wellington beats him proper this time, to make sure he stays down.

It all happens in Belgium.

And that's a weird thing, right – why's there a place in Belgium called Waterloo? It's two English words, innit? Maybe they call it something else over there. Probably named it after the train station in London where I noticed the other day you can now drop six quid on a fucking cheese roll. SIX QUID!

Or maybe they called it that cos that's where Napoleon shit himself.

As you were.

12 February 2025 – NOEL

Recording interviews with journalists today. They're doing the interviews now, in advance of the gigs – to go in the papers in a few months.

One of the little bastards asks: 'So, you always said you weren't in it for the money and that you would only re-form for the passion of the music.'

'Yeah,' I say.

'But you started by announcing a handful of gigs in the UK, and now it's a full world tour. Is that really not for the money?'

I examine the knee of my trousers and pick a piece of lint off it, flick it away. Then I look at the guy.

Here is a bloke, I tell myself, who has never had to hand his ex-wife a cheque for £35 million.

'If people want to buy tickets, who am I to turn *that* passion down?' I say calmly. 'And I'm not going to play for free.'

And I think: if Our Kid was in my position and got asked that, he'd probably have lamped him.

20 February 2025 – NOEL

Marcus came in today for another meeting. So many fucking meetings.

What's this one about?

'The media attention is intense,' he says. 'And getting madder by the week. Everything we do, there's paparazzi following us and papers trying to work out – are Oasis doing this or that, fighting or recording an album or whatever.'

'Standard,' says Liam.

'Well, we've got some time in the studio next week, and that's important for us. So, we've got a pretty radical strategy to distract the press.'

'Kill 'em,' says Liam.

'Less radical than that,' says Marcus. 'I was thinking: body doubles.'

Liam and I look at each other. For a moment I can't tell if we're going to laugh, or if it's a genuinely good idea.

'And here they are,' he says.

The door opens. And in walks a Liam followed by a Noel.

'We didn't just want cheap lookalikes who do party appearances, but properly crafted performances. We've auditioned and hired actors to perform as you.'

They shyly introduce themselves.

'We were thinking you should get to know each other this afternoon. We've got this time blocked out,' says Marcus.

'Alright,' says the Noel, looking at me. I feel a slightly strange sensation pass through me. 'Can I ask why you hold your guitar like that? It's interesting . . .'

'This guy looks like a prick, he's nothing like me!' shouts Liam.

But then I realise it's the actor portraying Liam who's spoken.

'Who the fuck do you think you are?' says Liam, pushing him. 'Get the fuck out!'

Within sixty seconds the Liams are kicking seven bells out of each other. Three chairs and six windows are broken, they've tumbled out the emergency exit into the alleyway, and there's the sound of someone's head being repeatedly bashed against a metal bin outside.

23 February 2025 – LIAM

Wake up with a hangover that feels like the Sex Pistols have been rehearsing in my head.

Look around to see my own dead body about three feet away.

What's going on?

Then I remember. It's that guy who's paid to look like me.

On first glance I thought, what the fuck, and felt a strong desire to punch him in the face for pretending to be me.

Ten minutes later, we were in the pub.

Can't quite work out the timings since then, but we seem to have been on a bender for thirty-six or forty-eight hours. Or two years maybe, fuck knows right now.

He's annoying, but a good lad.

Then I get a call from Marcus.

'You still alive?' he asks.

'Pretty sure I am. What happened to the other two?'

He explains that the two Noels spent a few hours shyly admiring each other and then played songs together for two days straight.

'Haven't seen him since yesterday but I think they're staring into each other's eyes and braiding each other's hair. It's fucking love at first sight, Liam!'

Fucking makes sense an' all.

20 March 2025 – NOEL

After selling a few million tickets, now suddenly we've got to take a close look at comps.

It's a political issue – who gets a freebie. As life goes on there's more and more people who you need to keep sweet. And as the gigs get closer, more people are asking for tickets, but they're already accounted for.

Difficult decisions need to be made.

People you don't want to piss off, and that.

Liam and I look over the seating plan for the first gig together.

'What's this?' I ask, pointing out a batch of seats.

Marcus looks over his notes.

'That's for your accountants. They're quite a big firm, actually. We offered them an allocation of twenty.'

'And this?' pointing at another block.

'Your financial advisors . . .'

‘And these six?’ asks Liam.

‘Your yoga instructor,’ says Marcus. ‘And her husband, her sister, and her sister’s fiancé, her mum and her dog walker.’

Liam and I exchange a look. We both sigh.

We are remembering the old days, when the only comps we gave out were to girlfriends and drug dealers.

‘Times have changed,’ he says.

‘What about these twelve?’ I say, pointing.

Marcus clears his throat and looks carefully along the list. ‘Those are for your drug dealers,’ he says.

Liam nods, looking satisfied.

‘He hasn’t got any drug dealers!’ I say. ‘He’s clean – just look at the whites of his eyes! Who are these actually for?’

‘None of them are dealers anymore,’ he admits. ‘Invited them for old times’ sake, you know.’

‘What they up to these days?’ I ask.

‘Erm,’ says Liam, itching his chin, and then counting them off on his fingers. ‘Financial advisor, accountant, yoga instructor, dog walker . . .’

‘OK that’s enough,’ I say.

1 April 2025 – NOEL

We agreed to do the concerts almost a year ago.

But when we agreed to go into the studio, we couldn’t be sure we’d have an album.

'Record it first,' I said. 'See what we've got. Then decide after.'

Everyone's pleased with it. It's mixed and sounding brilliant. And having recorded it first means we're in a stronger negotiating position.

So finally the time has come, and today, a couple of months before the first gig in Cardiff, we're at the office to sign the contract for the album.

It feels weird. Good, but weird.

As we're coming out onto the street – not a photographer in sight, thank fuck – I ask what made Liam finally call me.

'I guess I had to, after you'd written to me.'

'Me, write to you?' I ask. 'A likely fucking story.'

'Very funny,' he says. 'That email you sent.'

A funny feeling goes through me.

I look at him sideways.

'That's weird,' I say. 'I was just going to say, if you hadn't phoned I was going to call you. Because of the email *you* wrote *me*.'

He hasn't looked at me all this time, but now turns round to look me full in the face. I can tell he thinks I'm joking but doesn't understand why I would make a joke that's so unfunny. I'm giving him the same sort of look.

A tremble in my pocket distracts me. I pull out my phone.

'It's Mam,' I say. I put her on loudspeaker.

'Now, boys, have you signed today?' she says.

'Yeah,' says Liam.

'On the dotted line,' I say. 'There's some slight confusion about some emails, but apart from that, all's good . . .'

'Ah, now are you receiving ghost emails from each other?' she asks.

Liam looks at me and I look at him.

'What makes you say that?' I ask.

'Well now, I'm just an old Irish woman who doesn't know how to work a tablet, aren't I? So when I ask my son, he shows me how to use his tablet like the good boy he is. And if I ask two sons, they both show me, and if I ask them to show me how to log into emails, they both log into their own emails on my tablet.'

We're looking at each other like she's completely lost it.

'And then – imagine this – I've got access to both those sons' email accounts. And maybe each one sends the other a friendly email . . . and next thing you know . . .'

Liam says something loudly.

'That's bad language,' she says. 'Say ten Hail Marys. You should be thanking your old mother.'

'Two hundred million quid,' I mouth to Liam. He nods.

'Mother,' I say out loud. 'When we got to number one in the charts I offered to buy you a new house. And all you wanted was a new front gate.'

'I did,' she says.

'Well, how's about a new door knocker?' Liam asks.

'We can stretch to a new letterbox as well,' I say.

'Now don't go mad,' she says.

LIAM GALLAGHER'S HISTORY OF BRITAIN

Episode 4: The Nineteenth Century to the Present Day

1888–89 – Jack the Ripper

Nasty bastard serial killer stalks London women, like a *Silence of the Lambs* prequel but worse, but also without that scene where the bloke tucks away his jewels and does a little dance.

Just remembered there is already a *Silence of the Lambs* prequel. Where the lad from *Goodfellas*, who always wanted to be a gangster, eats his own brain. 'I always wanted to be a gangster,' he says. Can't get more gangster than eating a bit of your own brain, mate.

Anyway, this is worse than that. The killings are proper horrible and the women are mostly alcoholics who have been forced into prostitution. Basically, it's grim as.

And the fucker never gets caught. Not even Sherlock Holmes manages it.

And there's some juicy conspiracy theories about who it might have been. Some people say the Prince of Wales, or a famous painter or something.

But he never gets caught despite the fact they know his first name. Must be a lot of Jacks in London, I suppose.

But the police being fucking useless – some things never change.

1895 – The Trial of Oscar Wilde

So they send poor Oscar off to jail for copping off with another bloke – that's just not right. Fellers should be allowed to do what they want, you know. And so should birds an' all.

Bet he was popular in prison though.

Should of charged him for writing boring plays instead – that's a proper fucking crime. Then he'd have got a full life tariff with no chance of parole.

Died in Paris.

Like Jim Morrison. And Lady Di.

And Oasis, as it happens.

Not that there's a connection.

One that's been proved, at least.

1940 – The Battle of Britain

It's the summer after war is declared in 1939. Hitler's planes come over and start bombing the shit out of our airfields and radar. Looks like a sea invasion is about to happen.

OK, listen up. I actually watched a documentary about this so I know about it.

The Germans say to the British ambassador, why bother defending yourselves. Make peace with Hitler and he'll like chill out. But John Gielgud is like . . . No, wait, it's Ralph

Richardson. He's like: what am I doing? And the German ambassador (who is the bad guy from *The Spy Who Loved Me*) says: you appear to be holding up your fist and doing a rotating motion with your other hand and it's making your middle digit slowly rise up like ze clockwork. Was ist das.

And Ralph Richardson is like, yeah I'm telling the Fuhrer to go swivel, mate.

(And the German's like, well that wasn't obvious to me, etc.)

But then Laurence Olivier (who's in charge) is like, we've got Michael Caine and Robert Shaw and Christopher Plummer and loads of Polish pilots who we won't realise how good they are till later on. And things look pretty ropey for a bit but in the end we destroy loads of their bombers and things are OK.

1945–52 – Alan Turing and the Invention of the Modern Computer

A great British tragedy, man – cos this working-class lad managed to defeat the Nazis, and then helped build the first computers.

So he saved the world from tyranny and helped people look at unlimited boobs twenty-four-seven. Except he himself was not even into boobs.

That's irony.

In fact it was illegal to be a – a bloke what, you know, doesn't like birds. And the government cut his balls off and he topped himself.

Which I know is maybe not, like, the most sensitive or proper way to put it, but . . . that's what happened.

Tragedy.

Still – men around the world are raising a glass to you, Mr Turing. Hoping you're in Heaven. The real Heaven that is, not the gay club. But then, maybe there is a gay club in Heaven called Heaven.

Why not.

Fill yer boots.

NOTE FROM THE EDITOR

Dear Reader,

It is here that the entries (enigmatic as they are) abruptly stop. Are they a work of forgery intended to defame the Gallagher brothers? Or a true glimpse into what has been going on behind the scenes over the decades?

Legally I am obliged to tell you that the latter is not the case. For we can offer no proof. BUT IS IT THOUGH?

Again, the lawyer insists I say: no. Nevertheless, a tantalising glimpse into what may have been, for the author of these mysterious papers may have struck on the truth by sheer coincidence, or at least glanced across it. This strange individual's motives must remain as baffling as Noel Gallagher's sudden enthusiasm for reforming Oasis.

Perhaps one day the truth will be known.

S.P. (Editor)

ACKNOELEDGEMENTS

For the bolognese
1 tbsp olive oil
2 onions, chopped
2 cloves of garlic, sliced
3 carrots, chopped
4 sticks celery, sliced
900g beef mince
2 tins of chopped tomatoes
1 tablespoon Italian herbs
Worcester sauce
Tabasco sauce, to taste
Salt and pepper
3 rashers bacon, chopped (optional)
100g mushrooms, sliced (optional)
Glass of red wine (optional)

For the béchamel sauce
600ml milk
Bay leaf
3 cloves
1tsp whole pepper
50g butter
50g plain flour

1 packet of lasagne pasta
Handful of cheddar or parmesan cheese, or both

1. Put the oil in a large saucepan over a medium-high heat and add the onions and garlic. Stir and put the lid on to let them sweat for 4–5 minutes, taking the lid off to stir now and then.
2. Add the carrots and celery and sweat these for another 5 minutes.
3. Set aside the peel and cuttings of the onions, carrots and celery for later.
4. If you're using the bacon and mushrooms, add them now and fry until cooked through (4 minutes).
5. Take the lid off, tip n the meat and stir vigorously to break it up until it's changed colour (3–4 mins). Pour in the tomatoes, herbs, Worcester sauce, Tabasco sauce, 2tsp salt and lots of ground pepper (plus the wine if using), stir well, turn the heat to the second lowest setting, cover and let it bubble gently with while you do the rest, stirring every now and then (but make sure it cooks for at least half an hour and preferably a good bit longer).
6. Turn the oven on to 180 C.
7. For the béchamel, bring the milk to boil and put in the bay leaf, cloves, pepper and the peel and cuttings of the onions, carrots and celery. Turn off the heat and let the mixture infuse for ten minutes, then drain through a sieve and throw away the whole spices.

8. In a separate saucepan, melt the butter over a medium heat and then add the flour. Stir for 3 minutes so it forms a biscuit-coloured sludge and cooks through, then add the milk a splash at a time, stirring carefully to incorporate it to prevent lumps. Eventually you will be able to add the milk in a steady stream.
9. Turn the heat up high, bring the milk to a vigorous boil and keep it boiling, stirring all the time, until it thickens. It's quite hard to tell when this has happened but after stirring for a good 7–8 minutes it should be thickened. Take off the heat.
10. In a large baking dish, pour in a thin layer of lasagne then a thin layer of béchamel over it, and top with a layer of pasta (breaking up some sheets for the awkward corners). Repeat the layers in this order until you've run out of bolognese (hopefully at least three layers), and top with the last of the béchamel.
11. Sprinkle the cheese over the top and add a bit more ground pepper.
12. Bake for 45 minutes or until thoroughly bubbling and golden on the top.
13. Fucking have it.

ABOUT THE AUTHOR

Bruno Vincent is the author of more than thirty books. In 2018 he was indicted under the International War Crimes Tribunal and imprisoned on a small Pacific atoll from where he escaped on a raft made from palm leaves and human hair. He subsequently dug irrigation ditches in the Yucatán jungle and then (in 2023) broke the world record for blind-folded single-handed hang-gliding, above the Grand Canyon in Arizona. He established a chain of porridge restaurants in Canada in disguise as a large-breasted Scottish nanny, before settling in St Leonards on Sea, where he now lives.